Bandanas &
October Supplies

Also by M. Dylan Raskin

Little New York Bastard

Bandanas &
October Supplies

M. Dylan Raskin

THUNDER'S MOUTH PRESS
NEW YORK

BANDANAS & OCTOBER SUPPLIES

Published by
Thunder's Mouth Press
An Imprint of Avalon Publishing Group
245 West 17th Street, 11th Floor
New York, NY 10011

AVALON
publishing group incorporated

Copyright © 2006 by M. Dylan Raskin
First printing February 2006

Library of Congress Cataloging-in-Publication Data is available.

ISBN: 1-56025-753-9
ISBN 13: 978-1-56025-753-0

9 8 7 6 5 4 3 2 1

Book design by Maria Elias
Printed in the United States
Distributed by Publishers Group West

This book is dedicated solely to my mother,
Francine Raskin

I have the greatest memory you've ever heard of—I can't remember the last thing I forgot. With all the little white lies that I tell, I'd *better* have a good memory. It's fairly easy to get caught in a white lie if you aren't a sophisticated white-lie teller. The only real problem with white lies, as I see it, is that people get their noses so far out of joint when they find out they've been white-lied to. They get more out of joint over white lies than they do over big, *complicated* lies, in fact. It doesn't make any god-damn sense to me. In my opinion, generally speaking, an individual only lives one great story in his lifetime, and the rest is strictly for reminiscing purposes. If you're *older*, say, and clean out of things to reminisce about, then I don't think there's anything wrong with telling one or two little white lies to entertain someone. To the contrary, I find it to be fairly noble. The world is in severe shortage of good storytellers.

That's why when I told the security guards at Queens Hospital that I was having an agoraphobic attack, I didn't feel compunctious about it. I told them that I was an extreme agoraphobic and desperately needed to see Dr. Millani on the fifth floor. I figured that even if they didn't believe that agoraphobia business, they'd be so appreciative of my lie they'd let me go upstairs to see her anyway. They were always a pain in the ass at that place about letting you in to see a doctor without an appointment. Especially on Sundays. I must've been pretty convincing, though, because all they did was ask to see my driver's license and then they let me go upstairs. I was pretty surprised, to tell you the truth.

It was a Sunday and the fifth floor was closed to patients. I knew Dr. Millani would be in, though, because there was a medical conference being held there that morning. Nine times out of ten, I'm the last person in the world who would advocate barging in on someone at work—especially a doctor—but I was pretty anxious to see Dr. Millani. I wanted to say goodbye to her.

As I expected it to be, the fifth floor was empty and quiet. It was the most quiet I'd ever seen it. I didn't like the way it felt. It felt like the whole world was dead. There wasn't anyone working at the front desk, so I just went ahead and walked straight over to where Dr. Millani's office was. I stopped before I got to her door, though, because I heard her talking on the phone. I didn't want to be a nosey parker, so I made sure to stand a few feet back while she took her call. To be honest with you, I was already starting to feel sorry about being there. If there's one thing I can't stand, it's a person who shows up unannounced. I had half a mind to leave, but before I could I got caught up reading a sign on the wall. It was a cheap computer printout that said PAIN MANAGEMENT CHART, and underneath the slogan were ten faces, each with a different expression. For instance, the first face was smiling, and underneath it, it said, "No Pain At All." The *tenth* face was crying, and underneath it, it said, "Unbearable Pain."

It was a very morbid sign, if for no other reason than it was a cheap printout. If you're going to make a sign that's supposed to measure a person's level of pain, it should at least be a decent *looking* sign, in my opinion.

I didn't notice, but while I was wrapped up in reading that chart, Dr. Millani came walking out of her office. I guess she noticed me right away.

"*Hey,*" she said, very enthusiastically. She had a smile on her face that could've single-handedly lit up an Afghani cave. And she looked *good,* too. She didn't have her white doctor jacket on, for once. All she had on was a pink button-down and black pants. I hardly recognized her. It's a funny thing about doctors. You could see one of them every single day for a hundred years, but the second she takes off her white jacket you hardly recognize her.

Anyway, I was glad to see Dr. Millani. I hadn't seen her in a couple of months and was anxious to talk with her for a few minutes. She was very smart, Dr. Millani. She wasn't like a lot of these doctors you meet who are about as sterile as a goddamn gauze pad. She was very personable and everything, and very young and good looking. I'd bet dollars to donuts she's the best-looking doctor you've ever seen.

"I knew I'd find you here today, Dr. Millani," I said to her. I walked over and gave her a hug. She seemed pretty surprised to see me, that's for sure.

"I'm so glad you're here," she said. "C'mon, come inside." She meant her office. She was *always* inviting you into her office. That's why I liked her so much.

"Excuse the mess, Mike." She sort of laughed. I didn't see any mess.

I went over and sat in a chair opposite Dr. Millani and unzipped my jacket. Her office was about the size of a pack of smokes and it was Tarzan hot.

"I'm sorry to bother you on a Sunday, ace," I said and adjusted myself in the chair.

"Don't be ridiculous, Mike. I'm so happy you decided to stop in. You know, when we saw you drive off after—"

"Yeah, I know, I know, and I'm sorry about leaving that way. I just didn't know what else to do."

"I don't think anyone thought they'd ever see you again. I even tried calling your aunt's house a few times to find out how you were doing, but no one seemed to know where you were."

"I know it," I said. "I'm sorry for that. But that's why I'm here now, Dr. Millani." I zipped my jacket back up and adjusted myself in the chair again. That chair was making my ass go numb.

"Well, look," Dr. Millani said. "I know it's probably a stupid question, but I'm going to ask anyway—are you *doing* okay? I mean, are you handling everything all right? Do you need any *help* or any—"

"No, no, I'm doing all right. That's why I wanted to see you. I wanted to tell you that I'm going to fix everything very soon. I'm going to fix things and I wanted to say goodbye to you before then."

She was looking at me sort of funny.

"How're you going to fix things, Mike?"

I didn't answer her. I was too busy staring at a card Dr. Millani had on her desk. It had a squirrel on it, and the caption said: "Don't be nutty. Germs are everywhere . . . what have YOU touched today?" Next to the card she had a picture of her two daughters, who she'd adopted from China. I kept wondering if they were the ones who'd gotten her that card.

"Mike?"

"I'm sorry," I said. "I'm just tired from being away for so long."

Dr. Millani put her elbows on the desk and folded her hands.

"I had a feeling you weren't in New York," she said. "As soon as I saw you drive off I knew you were going to leave. Do you want to tell me where you've been?"

"You probably wouldn't believe me if I told you, Dr. Millani."

She was looking at me with an understanding face.

"Try me," she said.

Jitters in Lake George

The summer Sunday sun was, in one sense, the main attraction in Lake George that morning, but in another, all-too-familiar sense, the detail turning ordinarily nice vacationers into bastards. It was early—just after ten o'clock—and it was already cargo shorts weather. We were lucky, because my mom and I were sitting at a table in the most shaded corner of the tiny dining area at Mike & Don's Waterfront Café. Every few minutes, we'd see a sunburned vacationer walk into the restaurant and raise Cain on account of his breakfast not being ready. They were mostly people from the suburbs. I know suburban people when I see them—I can pick them out of a goddamn lineup.

It was the weekend before the Fourth of July, so naturally Lake George was crowded. You could hardly walk anywhere without tripping over someone, and all the restaurants and shops had lines out the door, even at ten in the morning. The lake was also crowded. You've never seen more speedboats and small cruise ships in all your life. And the *girls*. There were girls *every*where—good-looking ones, too. They were everywhere you looked—in cars, in stores, waiting tables, walking down the street, checking their tire pressure, waving their arms. They were practically coming out of the sky, for God's sake.

Mike & Don's Waterfront Café was my favorite restaurant in town. It was some small greasy spoon right on the lake, and their toast drove me crazy. From where we were sitting, my mom and I had a view of the lake that was more fiction than non. It was so bright and clear that morning you could practically read the addresses on the lakefront houses.

"See that log cabin house, Ma, about eleven o'clock?" I was squinting my left eye like I was taking aim with a rifle and pointing across the lake. "I was thinking about stopping over there later and putting a down payment on it—

but I'm going to tell them I'll only take the place if they remove the dock down by the water. Last thing I want is any *noise* outside our log cabin house, Mama."

My mom had a sort of half smile on her face, and she adjusted her dark sunglasses to get a better look at the house I was talking about.

"And then I'll tell you what I'm going to do, Ma. I'm going to go into town—over to the store that sells those custom Adirondack chairs, the one just past that battle cruiser on the corner—and I'm going to tell them that I need their *biggest* and most *expensive* Adirondack chair, and I'll give them top dollar for it if they paint a big bold *F* on it. A big bold *F* for Franny. *Then,* Ma, when it's ready, I'm going to take that Adirondack chair and rope-a-dope it to the back of Del, and I'm going to drive it over to our new log cabin house and put it right there on our big wraparound porch, so you can sit in it for as long as you want—all goddamn day and night if you feel like it—and look at the lake. And nobody else will be able to sit in that chair, Ma, because it'll have an *F* on it, for Franny. And even when you aren't around, I won't sit in it—I'll get my own chair, or I'll sit on the floor, or I'll just *stand* for all I care. What do you think, Ma?"

She didn't answer me. She just kind of sat there with the same half smile on her face. She knew I wasn't serious about putting a down payment on that log cabin house. I couldn't even afford to put a down payment on the Super 8 motel room we were staying in, for God's sake.

I took a bite of toast and wiped my face.

"You remember that weekend here last summer, Ma? You remember we were sitting right here, right at this same table, right around the same time as it is now—you were drinking that raspberry drink and I had a bottle of SoBe iced—"

"How is everything?" I heard someone behind me ask. It was Danielle, the hostess-waitress. She was standing behind me, just to my left, and looking like no other girl you've ever seen. She was wearing a black short-sleeve with blue jeans, and her dark hair was pulled back into a ponytail. Her hands were wet, probably from washing the counter, and the face of her commando watch was full of condensation. It all looked terrific. She was gorgeous in a summer sort of way, the kind of girl you could see yourself sitting next to in a resort town waiting for the trolley, the kind of girl who wouldn't turn many heads except yours, and would, more than likely, be more sought after by the sad, the downtrodden, and the unemployed than the masses. She was magnificent. She was summer.

"Swell," I said to her and wiped my mouth with a napkin. "They've got you running around like an eight-legged dog this morning, huh, ace?"

She paused for a second.

"Yeah, *every* morning," she said. "Are you here for the weekend or—"

"Probably. I want to try and find a place up here somewhere. I'm really pretty anxious to get the hell out of Queens already."

She paused again for a second. I couldn't take my eyes off her.

"I remember you telling me last summer you and your mom were trying to buy a house in town."

"Still looking," I said. "This place is like no place I've ever been, like no place I've ever *seen*. I can't imagine what it must be like to wake up here every day and see that lake. I mean, you never feel like a nuclear bomb is going to explode here any minute." I turned my head toward the water and sort of adjusted my sunglasses.

Danielle didn't say anything—she paused again. She might've been the most beautiful piece of summer left in the world, but she sure knew how to make you feel awkward the way she paused every time you said something.

"Anyway," I said. "You can't see anything like this *any-where* in New York City. In Queens or any other borough. And it's probably—"

All of a sudden I heard some loudmouth from inside the restaurant call out to her. She kind of rolled her eyes and said she'd be right back. I watched her walk inside and go into the kitchen. She looked terrific in her blue dungarees.

"Remember her from last summer, Ma?" I said and gave

my mom a pat on the leg. She was wearing blue jeans that had a Volkswagen patch sewn on the right side, and her short hair was getting tossed around in the breeze. I reached over and gave her a poke on the cheek just for the hell of it.

"You're lucky I don't pan your head in for ignoring me like this, Ma," I said jokingly. "C'mon, Franny May, give me the ole Spanish archer like only you can. Tell me to leave you the hell alone like you used to. Tell you what, Ma, if you tell me to screw off I'll run over to that little country store in the Village Mall, the one next to the post office, and I'll get you every single fleece blanket they have in there, every single piece of October in the whole store, so that come Octobertime, you'll be fleeced-out, just the way you like it. What do you say about that, Mama?"

I gave her a nudge with my elbow and then didn't say anything for a while. She just kind of sat there in her chair, with half her face covered in sun, the other half in shade, with her red, white, and blue Lake George fleece hooded sweatshirt on, and stared out at the lake.

We didn't stick around too long after that. The restaurant was getting too damn crowded, and the bees were starting to get on my last nerve. Just as we got up to leave, Danielle came over to us. I guess she saw us stand up.

"How was everything?" she asked. I got a charge out of it. It was the second time she'd asked us how everything was.

"It was great," I said. "Are you working all day?"

She paused again while she was cleaning our table.

"Yeah, I'll be here the whole day. My boyfrien—my *boss* is kind of understaffed, so . . ."

That drove me crazy. She was dating her goddamn boss. It seemed sort of sleazy, to tell you the truth. It's not so bad when you hear a *regular* girl tell you she's dating her boss, but when it's a girl like Danielle, it sort of makes you want to throw up. Anyway, I kept wondering if her son-of-a-bitch boyfriend-boss ever even noticed *once* how she paused before answering someone, or how her commando watch had condensation on its face and everything. I bet he never did, the bastard. And she *still* probably thought he was Mr. Charming.

"Well maybe we'll come back for dinner tonight," I told her. I knew we wouldn't. But I couldn't think of anything else to say. I was trying to conceal my disappointment about her having a boyfriend.

She paused again, naturally.

"Are you going to get your mom to come with you?"

"Yeah," I said. "We both think this place is terrific."

"Okay, well good luck finding a house. You know we get a lot of famous people here during summers."

During summers. I went crazy for that one.

"That Simon kid from that show on TV—what's it called again? The one where the father's a priest or something, and they have twins . . . I can't think of the name."

I laughed and told her I didn't know either. Normally I can't stand it when girls bang on about so-called famous people. But the way Danielle said it, it didn't bother me all that much.

"Well he was up here last summer—the Simon kid. I

think he moved into a house on the lake around Plum Island or somewhere."

I laughed again and said that whoever the bastard is, he probably doesn't deserve Lake George in the first place. Then my mom and I went inside to pay the bill.

"See you later, D.," I said as we were leaving.

"Bye!" she yelled over from the table she was cleaning "Tell your mom I said hi!" She hardly paused at all this time. I got a kick out of that.

It was still early and there wasn't much of anything to do. It was hot out and there were too many goddamn people around to make you feel like window-shopping. So after we left Mike & Don's Waterfront Café, we started heading over toward Shepard Park. Shepard Park is some little park that sits right in the middle of the Lake George village, and is, more than likely, unlike any other park you've ever seen. It's a park that, for uncertain reasons, looks and feels just as anonymous, just as *safe*, and just as fictitious on a sunny day in early July as it does on a shadowy day in late October. It overlooks the lake and is the sort of park you wouldn't mind walking barefoot through, the sort of park you can sit in with a bucket hat on your head and sunglasses on your face and feel like the most anonymous person in the world, like you're a million miles away from any nuclear bomb, like you're a million miles away from *everything*. It's very hilly and very tree-lined, and for one reason or another, *always* full of leaves, even in July, and the grass is always nice and green and short. But the real attraction at Shepard Park, at least as far as my mom is concerned, is the Adirondack chairs. Shepard Park starts—or ends, depending on how you look at it—at the top of Canada Street and stretches all the way down to the lake. Just before the water, though, they have these green Adirondack chairs—on the grass, under the trees, and in the sand. They aren't nailed down or anything, and you can move them wherever you want, but mostly they're just kept on the grass in the shade. Those chairs are what made my mother fall in love with Shepard Park. She can sit in one of those Adirondack chairs for five, six hours at a time, and you couldn't get her to move if you were coming at her with a cutlass in each hand.

Anyway, we went over by the bottom of the hill and each took a seat in an Adirondack chair right next to one another, facing the lake. I had my favorite dark blue bandana in one of my cargo pockets, and I took it out and tied it around my head the way I like. It was sunny as hell out and I could feel my arms and neck starting to burn.

"Hey, Ma?" I said. She didn't answer me but I knew she'd heard. "I just wanted to say, Ma, that I'm glad you're here with me this weekend. I'm just—I'm really glad you could make it. I don't know how I'd feel about this place if you—"

She was staring straight ahead, still looking at the lake, with her dark sunglasses on. Her left arm was on the armrest, and I saw that her hand, as it hung loosely from the armrest, was shaking. It was shaking uncontrollably.

I reached over and put my arm around her back and didn't say anything. It felt nice just sitting there with her, just the two of us, looking out at the lake from Shepard

Park, sitting in green Adirondack chairs. It felt safe. It felt like it *used* to feel.

Just like it always does during July, by around noontime Shepard Park started to get packed out. You could tell that most of the people walking around were on vacation, because a lot of them had camcorders and things, and most of them were hanging around by the lake taking pictures. I was starting to get a little antsy sitting there, to tell you the truth. I have a hard time just sitting around in a town like Lake George where there are more good-looking girls than you can shake a stick at. And besides that, I sort of felt like heading over to that country store I was telling my mom about, the one that sold the fleece blankets and things. The summer before, I'd gone into that place and met a girl who had the most terrific laugh you've ever heard. She really cranked my dial, and I was quite anxious to see if she'd be there again.

So I told my mom that I was going to take a walk into town and that I'd meet her back in the park in a little while. In just about any other place, I wouldn't have left her by herself, but I knew she'd be safe in Shepard Park, and I knew she didn't mind sitting there for a while. She could sit in that park until the day *Chryslers* are reliable.

Canada Street was starting to get pretty busy by the time I walked out of the park. Like always, there were a lot of motorcycles in town and a lot of good-looking girls walking around with their jerk-off boyfriends. I used to think that type of crap was limited to big cities where most of the people aren't human, but I was wrong because you see the same girls with the same lowlife guy-guys even in Lake George. It can drive you absolutely crazy. Mostly, though, there were a lot of families and tourists walking down Canada Street that day. You always saw a lot of them during the summer in Lake George, year after year. That's one of the things I liked most about the place. It was re*liable*. I've been to towns and places before that changed more times in a week than Lake George changed in a year. I hate that. I don't like when things change—it doesn't appeal a goddamn bit to me.

Anyway, I headed over to that country store that sold

the fleece blankets and other odds and sods. Like I was telling you before, the previous summer I'd gone in there with my mom and met a girl who, until I met Danielle from Mike & Don's, had ruined me for all other girls. She was working at the register, and we accidentally got caught up in a conversation when my shirt got stuck on one of the postcard displays. She was an aviation blonde from Jacksonville, Florida, with sort of wavy, curly hair— all greasy-looking and stuff—who was wearing a fleece hooded sweatshirt with blue jeans. No makeup or anything. Remember how I told you that Danielle was a summer sort of girl? Well Jacksonville was an *October* sort of girl. She was an October sort of girl if ever I've seen one. You could see her just sort of standing around in the fall, in a hooded sweatshirt and blue jeans, raking the goddamn leaves in her backyard. You could see how she'd be the type of girl who would go trick-or-treating with you on Halloween, even when she didn't want to, even when everyone else told her she was too old to go trick-or-treating. But what struck me most about Jacksonville was her laugh.

Her laugh was one for the books. It was a laugh that made *you* laugh, even when nothing was funny. It was a short, up-and-down-the-scale, out of place kind of a laugh—sort of goofy and childish—but with enough charm in it to keep a man up at night for months. It was the sort of laugh that, I'm reasonably confident, will have songs written about it someday.

It had been a year, but I was hoping that Jacksonville would be working at the country store again. I knew already, though, as soon as I walked into the Village Mall, that she was. It was very dark inside and I had my sunglasses on—I could hardly see a thing—but right away I heard that Jacksonville laugh coming from down the hall. She must find *everything* funny, because she was laughing long enough and loud enough for me to determine exactly which store she was in. And the funny thing was that when I walked in I saw that she was there by *herself*. She must be her own best comedian, that's for sure.

Anyway, she noticed me as soon as I stepped inside, and even before I said anything, she was laughing already.

"*Jacksonville*," I said.

"Hey, man," she said, laughing. She looked terrific, naturally. She was wearing dirty blue jeans with an undersized dark blue T-shirt, and it was perfectly obvious that she wasn't wearing an over-the-shoulder boulder holder because she looked like a goddamn peanut smuggler.

"You're back for another summer, huh, ace?" I said and took my sunglasses off.

"Yep." She let out another short up-and-down-the-scale laugh.

"That's gravy. I come looking for fleece blankets."

"For your mom?"

"Jesus Christ, Jacksonville, you have some goddamn memory. You remember last summer when we were in here lapping up all the fleece? You remember how *crazy* my mom was going for those fleece throws?"

"Yes I do," she said in a weird, playful voice, still laughing.

The thing about her that really sizzled my steak, aside from her terrific laugh and greasy hair, was that you could *tell* she'd never gotten ponced up or worn a dress or a skirt in her entire *life*. I'll bet you dollars to donuts she'll wear jeans and a T-shirt to her own goddamn wedding. And she had wonderful hands, too. They were sort of like Danielle's except Jacksonville wore one or two silver rings, and on her left wrist she had one of those homemade twine bracelets, which looked like it'd been run over by a truck about a hundred times.

"Well," I said, "you've got some memory, ace. You're like a sponge. It's incredible."

She was still laughing, of course. Short, up-and-down-the-scale laughs.

"Where's your mom?" she asked me.

"Over in the park. My mom can sit in that park until the day I can afford a house in this town. Or until hell freezes—whichever comes first."

She got a big charge out of that one and let go with one of the most enthusiastic cackles I've ever heard.

"I love that park," she said as she picked up some sort of necklace off the counter and hung it on one of the displays.

One thing about Jacksonville—as great a laugh as she had, she wasn't particularly long-winded.

"Yeah," I said. "No one ever asks you what your name is in that park. I mean, I can mix it up with someone in that park and tell her that I work in a Mobil Mart, and she won't even care. She won't even ask *ques*tions."

Like I expected her to, Jacksonville laughed her usual laugh and didn't say anything. I didn't care, really, except that I was starting to feel like a goddamn paralytic blabbermouth with me doing all the talking and her just laughing. The disappointing thing about girls is that they never want to have a conversation with you like they do in books and movies. In real life they never want to talk about *any*thing. To keep things from getting any more awkward, I went ahead and started looking for fleece blankets for my mom. I was also letting rip with some silent but violent ones, if you know what I'm talking about. I always wind up farting my brains out when I'm talking to a girl who really hoists my sailboat. I have one of those nervous stomachs.

Regardless, I found the fleece blankets I'd been looking

for in the back of the store. They were very *October* fleece blankets. Most of them had pictures of leaves on them—all different color leaves—and some had stars and things. I knew my mom would go nuts if she saw them, so I wound up grabbing three—two that had leaves, and a red one that had stars and planets on it. The only trouble was, I hardly had any cash on me. I never have any cash on me. I'm a mugger's worst nightmare.

"Hey, Jacksonville, you have any Adiós To Money machines around here?" I asked.

She was cackling away, naturally.

"There's one *waaay* down the street near the arcade. You know, across the street, if you make a left and go down by—"

"Yeah, I know where the arcade is," I said. I didn't feel like walking all the way down the street, though. And I probably didn't have enough money in my account anyway.

"All right, to hell with it," I said. "I'll just give you the goddamn credit card." Jacksonville laughed, of course. She was probably laughing at my stupidity.

I was all set to buy the fleece blankets when I noticed they had some bandanas for sale up near the counter.

"Hey, are these things soft or are they the cardboard type?" I asked her.

Jacksonville came closer to where I was standing so that she could get a better look at the bandanas. She looked even better up close. She had terrific arms.

"They're all right, I guess," Jacksonville said with a great north Florida accent. "You'll probably have to hang them from your porch if you want to really break them in." I was pretty sure she was marriage material after she said that.

I grabbed a few dark blue ones that weren't as soft as I like them, but Jacksonville had a face that I couldn't say no to, so I told her I wanted them plus the three fleece blankets. She was laughing. Again.

"Stuff for October," I told her.

"October supplies," she said as she bent down to grab a shopping bag from under the counter.

"You got that right, ace-face," I said. "Three more months."

"Yep," Jacksonville replied. More of that long-windedness that I was telling you about.

Anyway, she put everything in a bag and rang it up. I don't remember how much it came to, but it wasn't exactly cheap. I gave her the credit card because it was the only thing I had on me, just about.

"Francine Raskin. That your mom?" she asked me.

"Yeah, looks like she's buying. I'll owe her back for it and everything."

She was laughing again. That Jacksonville—she could sure make a guy feel like a real clever-clogs.

I signed the receipt and took the shopping bag off her.

"Thanks, Jacksonville. You going to be around for the rest of the summer up here or what?"

"Yep," she said, followed by a quick cackle. Jacksonville's famous last word: "Yep."

"Sounds gravy, ace," I said. "I'm sure I'll see you around." Truthfully, if Jacksonville was more of a talker that day, I would've looked for a way to sneak in my telephone number, but it's hard when you're talking to a girl who does more laughing than talking, and when you're stinking up the room with your disgusting farts.

"I'll see you, man," she said. "Say hi to your mom for me." My mom must've made some impression on her, that's for sure. It's funny, too, because I only remember them talking for about five minutes.

"Sure will," I said, and started walking out. I was mad at myself already for not asking her on a date, or at least asking if she'd meet me out for an intellectual conversation or something like that. I'm *still* mad at myself. The trouble is, I only have pluck about fifteen days out of the year. The rest of the time I'm about as silent as an Enron executive. It's really quite a situation. Anyway, when I was just about out of the Village Mall and onto Canada Street, I heard Jacksonville start laughing again. I must have missed the joke.

Canada Street was even more crowded by the time I got out of Jacksonville's store, so I decided to walk down the alley near Christie's—another lakefront restaurant—and just cut across to the park. It was more scenic that way.

When I got down near the end of the alley, I turned left
and started walking along the water toward Shepard Park.
But on the way, I couldn't believe what I saw. Coming in
my direction was a wolf pack of about ten girls—ten suburban *prissy* girls—all linked arm in arm and carrying so
many shopping bags I think they were slowly sinking all of
Lake George. I always know suburban prissy girls when I
see them. They all look exactly the same. They all wear the
same colorful, trendy clothes and have perfect teeth, and
they never have any pimples on their faces. I can't stand
them. I don't trust a girl who doesn't have at least one or
two pimples on her face.

Anyway, this wolf pack was taking up nearly the entire
sidewalk, and they were all giggling and singing "LA
Song" in a sort of upbeat, *giggly* way. For some reason, it
made me think of something that happened a couple of
summers ago. It was sometime in August, I remember,
because it was just a few days after my mom's birthday. The
two of us were on vacation in Lake George, and right after
lunch we went over to Shepard Park. We were walking

uphill through the park in order to get to Canada Street, I remember. My mom was so tired and weak she couldn't make it up the hill by herself, so she asked me to stand behind her and *push* her up it.

"Just keep moving your legs, Ma," I kept telling her. I had my hands on her back, and she just sort of leaned her weight on me.

"What'd Dr. Millani say to you on the phone today?" she asked me. She asked so low I could hardly hear her.

"Nothing really. She just said that we should probably take it easy for a few days and not think about anything. She said that you're probably stressing yourself out and—"

"Did she give you the *results* is what I'm asking you, Mike. You know that's what I meant."

"I didn't even ask her, Ma. Look, I'm sure if she was con*cerned* about something she would've said so. So why don't you just try and enjoy—"

"That's real easy for *you* to say, Mike, you're not the one who's—"

"What the hell are you *talking* about, Ma? You know

damn well that whatever concerns *you* concerns me as well. There's no separation here. But I'm sure that if she was concerned about something, she'd have said something to me."

"So she didn't say *anything* to you about my blood test? Really?"

"*Really*. But she did say we should buy a house up here as soon as possible. She says it'd be good for your health."

"Yeah, sure."

"I'm serious, Ma. That's what she said. She said we should get a house right on the lake, right near the—"

"And where would you like me to get the money from? I can't exactly become a *hooker*, Mike. What man is going to want a fifty-three—"

"All right, knock if off, would you? All I'm saying is we should get out of New York before the—"

"I know, I know. Before the nuclear bomb explodes, I know."

"Well, yes, now that you mention it. That's as good a reason as any, don't you think? Besides, Ma, *look* at this place. You know how much less *stress* we'd both have if we were living in a nice, quiet, *safe* town like this? I mean, seriously, Ma, you should really—"

"Wait, Mike, I can't—"

She just sort of dropped the anchors and stood still for a minute.

"You can't make it any further, Ma?"

She shook her head no.

There was a bench a few feet from where we were standing, so I managed to get her over to it. We sat down and didn't say anything for a while. My mom kept her head back and tried to catch her breath.

"Want me to carry you to the car, Ma?" I asked her.

She kind of laughed, in an out-of-breath sort of way. "You couldn't if you tried."

"Sure I could," I said. "What do you weigh, about a hundred and forty?"

"It's okay. Just give me a minute to get my strength back. Okay? Just give me a minute."

We sat there for a few more minutes without talking. I

sort of sat crouched over with my elbows on my legs, and my mom kept her head back trying to catch her breath. All of a sudden, while we were sitting there, I heard her start reciting the words to the "I shall not die" prayer. It was hard to even *hear* her. She was saying it sort of sotto voce, with her head leaned back.

"O give thanks to the Lord, for He is good. His steadfast love endures forever. Let Israel say, 'His steadfast love endures forever.' The right hand of the Lord is exalted, the right hand of the Lord does valiantly. I shall not die, but I shall live, and recount the deeds of the Lord. The stone which the builders rejected has become the head of the corner. This is the Lord's doing. It is marvelous in our eyes."

"What are you doing, Ma?" I said.

She didn't answer me. All she did was sit there and keep on going with her prayer business.

"Hey, Ma, are you all right? You're starting to worry me over here."

She just kept on going, saying it over again.

"*Ma?*"

"*What*, for God's sake?"

"What are you doing, huh? Are you trying to scare me half to—"

"Calm down, Mike, would ya? Aren't I entitled to—"

"Entitled to *what*, Ma? To scare me half—"

"Aren't I *entitled* to start feeling like things are looking up? Huh? Close your eyes for a minute, Mike. C'mon, put your head back and close your eyes for a minute.

"Ma—"

"Just do what I say. C'mon."

I leaned my head back and closed my eyes. The sun was so bright I could see it through my eyelids.

"Now," my mom said. "Don't you feel better?"

I didn't answer. I just kept looking straight up.

"Isn't everything looking up now? Huh? I think we've just changed our luck, Mike. Things are finally looking up."

I was thinking about that while the pack of prissy suburban girls were walking toward me giggling their way through "LA Song." Only spoiled suburban girls who don't have a care in the world other than their love lives would take a sincere song like "LA Song" and turn it into a giggling cheesefest. But regardless, I kept thinking about my mom sitting on that park bench and reciting the "I shall not die" prayer. I kept thinking about her trying to memorize it. I could just picture her sitting at home and reading it off the back of an envelope a thousand times before she got it just right, before she reached the point where, without looking, without holding her eyes open, she could recite it to herself without a single mistake. I could picture her asking God to help with her memorization of it, to help with her delivery, and to see to it that the "I shall not die" prayer was not used in vain, or in satire, even in times of great joy and celebration.

Anyway, I had to make sure I got out of the wolf pack's way before they ran me over. I practically had to jump into the goddamn lake to avoid being flattened.

After they got by me, I started heading over to the park. I saw my mom sitting in the same spot she was in when I left her, still in her green Adirondack chair, still staring at the lake in that nice, perfect, *compact* way. I walked over and sat down in the chair next to her and set my shopping bag down on the grass.

"Hey, Ma," I said. "Got a surprise for you." I took out the red fleece blanket that had all the stars and planets on it and everything. "I bought this from Jacksonville over at that country store. She told me to say hi to you, and I said I would, so hello from Jacksonville."

I put the fleece blanket down on her chair so she could have a better look at it. She just kept staring straight ahead at the lake.

"Just wait until October, Ma. Just wait. We're going to have more October supplies than anybody on our block. And you know what we're going to do on Gate Night? We're going to have a horror movie marathon. We're going to watch every single spooky show we own—all those eighties movies we like that don't have forty minutes of previews and the product placement crap. And then we'll build a gigantic *fleece* blanket fort right there in the living room, okay, Ma?"

She still had that red fleece blanket sitting next to her, and I put my arm out and gave her a pat on the back, just for the hell of it.

"We're going to be all right, Ma. Don't you worry. You see that lake out there?" I pointed at the water. "I'm going to get us a house right on that lake one of these days, I promise. Because if there's one thing I know, Franny, if there's one thing I'm *pos*itive about, it's that there's nothing wrong with aiming high in this crazy goddamn life. But anyway, what we'll do is, every time it thunders and lightnings, we'll sit on the porch in our Adirondack chairs, but we won't *say* anything, we'll just sit there feeling safe and cozy and listen to the thunder, and when it stops, we'll take a walk down to the water and skip rocks just the way we used to do when I was a kid and we'd all go camping. You remember when I was a kid and had astraphobia? I don't have it anymore, Ma. I've outgrown it. I'll sit outside with you for ten hours during a thunderstorm, if you want me to."

My mom was looking at me with her dark sunglasses

on, but the sun was shining in such a way that I could see right through them.

"My eyes are still yellow, Mike," she said.

"They won't be for too much longer, Ma. You remember what I told—"

Before I could finish my sentence a horn blared that was so damn loud I nearly jumped out of my New Balances.

"Jesus Christ," I said. "That son of a bitch gets me every time, Ma. You remember last summer? Every time that horn blared I jumped. Every single time. Do you remember that? That ship always gives me the jitters. Always."

That horn was from a cruise ship called the *Minne-Ha-Ha*. It was always docked in Lake George and it went out about two hundred times a day to give people a tour of the lake. And every time it left the dock, and every time it returned, it blew its horn. And every single time—no matter how many times I'd heard it—it made me jump.

"There she goes, Ma." I started waving at the ship, and at all the people standing on deck. Most of them waved back, too. "Go on, Ma, wave at them."

My mom started waving. "Oscar," she said, sort of childlike and sweet. "Looks like a big Oscar in the water." Oscar was a rather large fish I had when I was a kid.

"Yeah, you're right, it does, Ma." I put my head close to hers and gently put my forehead to her left cheek. "You remember what I told you the other day?" I said very quietly. "You remember how I told you that we were going to get out of Queens and never look back? And I told you that things were going to get better because, heaven help us, Ma, we're not like anything else, we're not like anyone else they've ever seen. Well look where we are," I said, and I turned toward the lake and watched the *Minne-Ha-Ha* float by, my right check pressed against her left cheek. "We've come a long way, Ma, a long way from Sixty-eighth Drive, and one of these days we're going to live in this town and we're going to leave *everything* behind, and when people wonder where we are, we'll just let them wonder, and we'll only call when *we* want to call, or we just won't keep a damn phone at all. Anybody who wants to get in touch with us will have to write us a letter—and if we don't feel like opening letters for a month, then we won't. And *nobody*, nobody will be able to tell us differently, because we'll be far away, Ma. We'll be so safe and far away that even when Manhattan is attacked with nuclear bombs we won't even know about it, and when gas prices go up to twenty dollars a gallon, we won't hardly care, because we'll be so far away from everything and tucked away in this little safe place that it won't even matter to us. We'll get a motorcycle, how about that? A little Honda motorcycle that's reliable and never breaks down and gets about a hundred miles per gallon. We'll hardly ever have to buy gas again, and we'll just use Del in the wintertime. I bet if you had a Honda and you lived in this town, it would run for a million miles and never stop. I bet if we moved here tomorrow and never left, Del would run until the speedometer ran out of zeros. And imagine this place in late October, Ma, right around Halloween. I bet this town looks *spooky,* like a real old-fashioned Halloween town. My God, I get the jitters just thinking about it. We could build fleece blanket forts every night during October. And instead of having wallpaper or painting the walls, we'll just hang up big old blankets—on the walls, on the ceiling, *everywhere*. That way it'll *always* feel cozy inside, even in the spring and summer. And the *fires*—imagine the fires we'll make in our fireplace during December. And come New Year's Eve, when the *Twilight Zone* marathon is on, we'll wear fleece pants and watch every single episode. I'll invite Jacksonville over and she'll watch with us—she'll probably be laughing the whole time, but at least it'll be a *good* laugh—and when the ball drops, we'll all start jumping up and down and singing those New Year's songs that you used to play on the piano all the time. Or we'll sing some of that Jennie DeVoe stuff you like so much. We'll all sing those songs and jump up and down until we get too tired, and then Jacksonville and I will go sleep in one of our blanket forts, and you'll go sleep in your bed, because I know with your bad back you won't want to sleep in the fort with us, and besides, if Jacksonville is feeling a bit *randy* I won't particularly mind accommodating her. *Oh,* and I almost forgot about Christmastime! I'll go out and pick up a few pies from Pizza Jerks, and we'll eat pizza and watch George Bailey lasso the moon. You can wear your Lake George fleece hooded sweatshirt—this one, the one you're wearing now—and I'll wear my favorite sweater, the one that looks better inside out, the one with the hole in its sleeve, and I'll tie one of my favorite blue bandanas around my head, just the way I like it, and we'll keep all the lights off except for the kitchen, and we'll watch the snow coming down through the living room window, and I'll go ahead and make some hot chocolate—I won't even care if it gives me ten thousand zits—and I'll make you some of that green tea you like so much, and we'll sit on the couch with all our fleece blankets and throws and pillows around us and watch the snow, and if you want I'll tell you a story. The kind of stories I used to tell you when I was a kid and all of us used to go camping—do you remember that? I used to try and scare you and Dad by telling you urban legend stories, and boogeyman stories, and even though you knew all of them already, you *always* pretended like you were hearing them for the first time. And do you remember what Dad used to say? *'They're coming for you,*

Franny. They're coming to GET you, Franny.' God knows I can hear that clear as day, Ma, just like it was yesterday, just like it was an *hour* ago. Anyway, when we get our little Lake George house we'll do all those things, Ma, and you won't have to worry about anything being yellow again, okay? For the love of God, we're aiming high."

I heard my mom whispering something, but I couldn't make it out at first.

"What, Ma?"

She kept on whispering, and I could see that behind her sunglasses her eyes were closed.

"Twenty dwarfs taking turns . . ." she was saying, though I couldn't make the rest out.

"I can't . . . what're you saying, Ma?" I leaned my head in to listen more closely.

"Twenty dwarfs taking turns doing handstands on the carpet. Twenty dwarfs taking turns doing handstands on the carpet. Twenty dwarfs taking turns doing handstands on the carpet . . ."

I could barely hear her. But I didn't say anything else

about it. Instead, I put my arm around her back, kissed her on the head, and told her that Lake George wasn't the same without her.

Carlin Park and the Flying Fish

O ne thing about South Florida in the summer—it can sure remind a guy what it's like to be old, even when he's young, even when he's still light on his feet. It might have something to do with the weather, especially during the daytime when the air is so thick and humid you could swear you're experiencing the blast wave from a nuclear explosion. It's not just the weather, though. It seems to me, if you're in South Florida in the summer, odds are you aren't there because you *want* to be there, but because, for one reason or another, you *have* to be. In my personal estimation, there are few places on earth more tailor-made for hiding yourself away—for disappearing for a while.

At least that's how it felt in Palm Beach Gardens by one o'clock. The sun was so strong you could hardly hold your eyes open. Sitting on that curb outside of Sears, my mom and I were both sweating like nobody's business, taking turns fanning out our shirts and wiping our brows.

"I'd love to know what the hell is taking so long," I said to her and wiped my forehead with my sleeve.

My mom had a white button-down on that was wrinkled something awful. I liked the way it looked, though. It made her look young, especially with the black cargo shorts she was wearing. I'd made her buy them a few summers ago on account of a gift certificate I'd gotten as a present. At first she didn't care for them all that much, but after she discovered how useful the cargo pockets are, she changed her opinion.

"Do you remember the last time we were here together, Ma? We were sitting inside, right near that place with the organic fruit drinks. I remember that day like it was yesterday, Ma. I can even tell you what I was wearing."

My mom had her face tilted up toward the sun.

"You know what that says up there?" I said while pointing upward. "That blue swimming pool of a sky says that you and I are twelve hundred miles away from every goddamn thing under the sun, Ma. We're so far from reality right now we're lucky if we don't get attached to all of it. But the best part of it is, Ma, we're not—"

"Mr. Raskin?" someone called out behind me. It was the Sears mechanic, a real dipstick if I ever met one. "I'm sorry for keeping you waiting, buddy. We only got three guys working. You still want those Michelins or—"

"Yeah, the seventy-dollar Michelins, not the hundred-dollar ones." The son of a bitch had tried to hoodwink me earlier by telling me the only tires they had for my particular Honda were hundred-dollar Michelins.

"You got it, boss," he said. "You might want to go hang out inside for a few hours. We got eight cars ahead of you."

I wasn't too thrilled about leaving my car with those bastards, but since I needed new tires pretty badly I didn't make a stink about it. I gave the son of a bitch my keys and told him I'd be back around five to pick it up.

I always know when I'm in the Palm Beach Gardens Mall. You could blindfold me, lock me in the trunk, drive me around for two weeks, drop me off there, and I'd *still* be able to tell you where I was. It has a certain smell, sort of an artificially tropical, *air-conditioned* smell. And it's always cold as a bastard inside. They always have the air-conditioning on too high, and even on days when it's ninety-five degrees outside, you have to wear a sweatshirt. I can't stand that. I'd rather sweat half to death than be frozen by air-conditioning.

It had been a while since I'd been there, and I'd forgotten just how many Lord Mucks there were in that place. You've never seen more silver watches and collared shirts in the same place at the same time, and the private school uniforms were coming at you from every which way but Sunday. The private school sewage was *always* running rampant in there, yelling into their cellular phones and carrying keys to very big-shot cars. If there's one group of people that makes me sick, it's rich private school kids. None of them have any goddamn class.

My mom and I walked in and took seats that were at a table in the food court but close to the exit doors. Both of us were turning blue by the time we sat down, because it was about ten degrees in there.

"You remember the last time we came here together, Ma?" I said. She had her sunglasses on, naturally, and I kind of reached over the table and gave her hand a whack. "It was in January, I remember, and we were escaping the cold. I can still remember speeding down I-95 and feeling the air gradually getting warmer and warmer. Do you remember what you said to me the first time we came to this place, after we parked at the back end of the parking lot? It must've been seventy-five degrees, the most perfect weather you can imagine, and we got out of the car, and you said, in sort of an overdramatic, *poetic* way, 'Peace be mine.' You had your arms out and you were tilting your face up toward the sky. Do you remember that, Mom? Now that I think about it, I only wish I'd had a damn camera on me. I would've taken your picture, folded it over twice and stuck it in a mason jar where—"

All of a sudden, straight out of left field, I heard a girl say "*Dylan?*" If there's one thing I can't stand, it's when some pain-in-the-ass sticks her nose in the middle of a conversation you're trying to have with your mother.

I knew who it was right away. I didn't even have to look up. Her name was Michelle, and I'd met her a few years ago in that mall. She worked at the bookstore, and I'd see her every time I went in there. She was purely high-society excrement—the type who was always banging on about what big-shot college she wanted to go to and how many times she'd been to Europe. I always know I'm dealing with a high-society, suburban blowhard when she tells me about how many times she's been overseas. I can't stand that type of thing. First of all, I don't understand people who've seen all of another country but have never seen *any* of their own. Nine times out of ten, when some good-for-nothing suburban socialite tells you that she's been to Australia, for instance, it's a bulletproof bet that she's never been out of her own backyard otherwise. She may have been to every country in the world that starts with an A, but you can take it to the bank she's never been to Alabama and watched the sun set. You can take it to the bank she's never even *thought* about going to Alabama. I don't understand it at all. I'm not even so sure I want to.

Anyway, Michelle was standing so close to our table she was practically dancing on top of it.

"Hey there, ace," I said. I didn't bother taking my sunglasses off. I didn't want her to pull up a goddamn chair or anything. "Been a long time."

"I *know*," she said. "How *are* you?" She sounded *very* chipper. These socialites are *always* chipper.

"Fine. I've been doing—"

"You know I almost didn't recognize you," she said. "You buzzed your head!" Then she ran her dirty hand over my head like she was my number one best bud.

"Yep, I did. Had to. Part of the protocol." She was looking at me like I had a booger coming out of my nose or something. I figured I'd just lead her up the garden path a little. "I joined the Marines."

"That's fan*tastic*," she said. Fantastic—I got a charge out of that one. "Aren't they feeding you, Dyl? You look like you're ninety pounds."

I laughed a little at her goddamn nerve.

"Yeah, well that's what eating healthy will do to you, ace," I said. "It'll kill you slowly. Anyway, never mind *me*. What're *you* up to? You still over at the bookstore?" I figured I'd change the subject a little. Suburban girls drool all over themselves when you ask them personal questions.

"Just for the summer," she said. "I'm going back to school in August."

"Sounds gravy, Mish."

"So what're you doing down here, Dyl? Did you move back down or are you—"

"No, nothing like that. I'm just down here spending some time alone with my mom, that's all. My car's over at Sears getting some new tires put on, so I've got about four hours to kill."

It was so cold in there I was practically showing the beginning signs of pneumonia.

"So what's your mom doing? Is she shopping for—"

"Hey, listen," I said. "You know that park up in Jupiter,

about eight miles or so north of here? *Carlin* Park. Are you familiar with it at all?"

"You mean the one on A1A? By the beach?"

"Yeah. It has that really great parking lot that always empties out after five o'clock, and there's that pond over there in the park. You know the pond I'm talking about? The one that has those fish that fly out of the water every few seconds?"

"Fish that fly?" She had a look on her face that I wish you could've seen. All suburban girls get the same look on their face when you ask them a question about somewhere other than Europe.

"Yeah, you know the ones that—"

All of a sudden her goddamn cellular phone rang. She had one of those phones that played a song when it rang. If there's one thing that can make me want to lose my lunch, it's that. Anyway, she walked away from us and took her call.

"You see this type of excrement, Ma? This is the type of—"

"Sorry about that," Michelle said. It was the quickest goddamn phone call I'd ever seen. "That was my manager. I've got to get over to the store. Stop in and keep me company. I'll be there all day."

"Sure will, ace. I'll come by in a little while."

"Okay. I'll see you in a little while then. Tell your mom I said hi."

"Semper fi," I said.

While she was walking away from us I saw her reach for her cellular phone again. I got a kick out of that.

The only thing I liked about that mall was that they had a place in there that sold these organic fruit drinks. They made them right in front of you, and they had any kind of fruit you could think of. My favorite was the Orange Sensation. It was also my mom's favorite. Naturally, it was one of the most expensive drinks on the menu, but it didn't matter because it was one of the best drinks in the world. After Michelle walked away from us, I got up and bought a large Orange Sensation and brought it over to my mom.

It was still early and I had practically another three

hours to waste. I could tell that my mom was tired, so I figured I'd just go over to the bookstore to see if I could pick up a book I'd been looking for. I'd been looking for a copy of *The Losers' Club* by Richard Perez for a few months without any luck. Goddamn bookstores—they don't carry anything worth your while. The only things they stock are big-shot books by big-shot writers.

So I told my mom I'd be back in a little while and she should just take it easy in the food court and drink her Orange Sensation. She didn't seem to mind, so I headed over to the bookstore. There were so many Lord Mucks and Lady Mucks in that place that it was just about impossible to walk anywhere without tripping over somebody. I didn't particularly mind, though, because I was able to get lost in the crowd without Michelle noticing me right away.

The fiction section was lousy with mass-market paperbacks and all sorts of mainstream, safe, uninspired books. You couldn't find a single book in that place that took any sort of *risk*. I like a book that takes at least *some* risk, for God's sake. I'm not saying it should be a goddamn exposition fair or anything, but it should at *least* be distinguishable from what the masses are reading. The masses don't read anything worth a damn.

Anyway, I couldn't find *The Losers' Club*, so I figured I'd go up to the register and ask Michelle if she'd do a computer check for me. I waited a little while, though, until the line got shorter. There were more Lady Mucks and preppies in that place than you could shake a stick at, and every few seconds you'd hear some brainwashed soccer mom going nuts over one of these big-shot diet books. I got a laugh out of it.

Michelle noticed me before I even made it to the register. She was working with some fat older woman who looked like she wouldn't be able to tell a good book from the last owner's manual she read. I don't understand how some people get jobs in bookstores. I swear to God I don't.

"*Dyl!*" Michelle yelled at me. She kept calling me Dyl. You'd think I was a goddamn pickle, for Christ's sake.

"Hey," I said. "I felt compelled to stop in to see if you could do a book search for me."

"And I thought you came to visit me," she said, and kind of laughed.

"I *did*—only I'm killing two birds with one stone." I paused for a minute to try and keep a straight face. "I'm looking for a book called *The Losers' Club*. You ever hear of it?"

"I don't think so," she said with a quizzical look on her face. "Hey, Kim?" She was talking to the fat older woman. "Did you ever hear of *The Losers' Club*?"

Not that I was expecting her to say yes or anything, but all *Kim* did was shake her head no. I wasn't sur*prised*, but she could've at least pretended to have had a goddamn personality.

"I don't think we have that one, Dyl. What's it about?"

"It's about a writer who can't get published. Do you do special—"

"Isn't that the whole point of *writing*, though?" she said. "If you can't get published can you really call yourself a writer?"

I wasn't surprised that a spoiled suburban socialite like

her had said that. I replied that, in my opinion, some of the world's best writers are unpublished writers, and that if a poor bastard has just spent the last nine months of his life holed up in a closet in front of a typewriter, hating every second of it, and for reasons that aren't fully recognizable even to him, he plans to do it all over again, then he's already earned the right to be called a writer, whether or not he has the wherewithal to get published. I told her that the only difference between a published writer and an unpublished writer is that the published writer will forever walk around without pants on, and will, in *most* cases, die a very poor, unhappy, unfulfilled son of a bitch with ten-cent royalty checks protruding from his coffin. Other than that, I said, there isn't a goddamn difference between the two.

You could tell that ole fatso standing next to Michelle was getting annoyed. She kept asking Michelle if she was being paid to socialize. It was very funny to me, and after Michelle's verbal diarrhea about unpublished writers, I'd be lying if I said I didn't experience a twinge of schadenfreude.

In any case, I asked Michelle if she'd special-order *The Losers' Club* for me. I told her that even if I wasn't around to pick it up when it came in, she should just stick it somewhere in the fiction section.

I was just about to leave, to head back over to the food court to see my mom, when I remembered those flying fish at Carlin Park.

"Hey, Mish," I said. "About that park up in Jupiter, the one with the pond."

"Mmm-hmm?"

"Well, is that a *common* thing down here—flying fish? I mean, is that a *Florida* thing, or am I way off base here?"

"I've never heard of anything like *that* before, Dylan. Are you sure they're—"

"You know what?" Michelle's manager, Kim, cut in. "Are you talking about a place in *Jupiter?*"

"Yeah," Michelle said. "You know that park on A1A?"

"Well, I'm *from* Jupiter and I've never heard anything about no flying fish. You know what? That doesn't even make any *sense.*"

Kim was one of these mentally irregular people who starts every sentence with the question *You know what?* If there's one thing that can grate on my last nerve, it's that. Every single pain in the ass these days throws at least *two* "you-know-whats" into every sentence they speak. It can really drive you crazy. I don't know how it doesn't drive *them* crazy, to be perfectly honest with you.

Anyway, I thanked them both for their time and said I'd come back in a few days to see if the book was in. I didn't feel like wasting my breath asking them anything more about Carlin Park and the flying fish because people like them never know about things like that. They never know about anything worthwhile.

After I left the bookstore I walked back over to the food court. It was very crowded and very bright. The ceiling was transparent, and it let in too much goddamn sun. You could hardly find a spot that had any shade. I walked straight to the front of the food court near the doors and saw my mom sitting at the table where I'd left her. She was drinking her Orange Sensation through a purple straw, and I pulled up a chair and sat down. She still had her sunglasses on, and there was so much sun coming in from the window next to her, she was practically glowing. I wish to God you could have seen her. She looked so perfect and anonymous you just wanted to watch her for hours, without even saying anything, without even *doing* anything. You just wanted to watch.

"You want a sip?" she asked when I sat down.

I laughed slightly. "No thanks, Ma. You enjoy it. Been a while since we've been here together, huh?" I sort of looked around a little. "You remember what happened last time, Ma? You wanted to go into that store to look for shower radios, and I wanted to wait outside and sit on the roof of the car to get some sun, and while I was out there, one of those dirty keystone cops told me that I looked like an eyesore and wasn't allowed to just sit there on the roof like that. I remember when I finally found you downstairs, right near FAO Schwarz, on that bench—the one with the wishing well behind it. You were just sitting there with your two packages next to you, singing that DeVoe song.

You remember the one? God, how does it go? I can't think of it. I can hear the melody but I can't think of the words. Anyway, I just remember how safe I felt when I finally found you. I felt just like that time in high school when you came to parent-teacher night, just after Dad died. I had the same feeling. And I couldn't even *tell* you how many times I've . . ."

My mom slowly put her cup down on the table, then used her right hand to hold the purple straw in place so that she could take a drink. But the way the sun was coming through the window to my right, her hand—the one holding the straw in place—looked slightly yellow, just slightly off-color.

I wasn't sure quite what to say.

"There're flying fish waiting for you at Carlin Park, Ma. We'll go there soon, okay? We'll go there very soon."

Walking outside into the Florida sun, just after four o'clock, it was impossible to avoid a feeling of lethargy. The two of us dragged our heels around the mall until we got to Sears. I figured I'd ask if the car was ready yet.

When we walked in, I noticed that the dipstick who'd taken my order earlier wasn't there anymore.

"Can I help you, sir?" the son of a bitch behind the register asked me.

I told him I was there to pick up my car and gave him my name.

"The del Sol, right?"

"Yeah. I had new tires put on it. Is it ready yet? I've really got a lot of things to—"

"Yeah, it's all set for you. Does that thing have a VTEC in it?"

"Nah," I said. These rednecks are always asking what type of engine you have in your car.

"Any chance you'd be interested in selling it? For a car that has 120,000 miles on it, it runs like it's brand new."

I kind of laughed. "No thanks," I said. "I don't go anywhere without that car. And, God willing, if gas prices stay under twenty dollars a gallon, I won't have to."

He laughed and rang me up. The bill came out to damn near three hundred bucks, which, naturally, was a lot more than I had on me. I told him I'd just pay with a credit card.

He was all set to finalize everything when all of a sudden he stopped.

"Whose credit card is this?" he asked me.

"It's my mother's, why?"

"Well, it says Francine Raskin on it, and I'm not supposed to allow you to use someone else's—"

"Listen, man," I said. "The last thing my mom cares about is whether or not I use her credit card. You don't have to worry about that. Besides, you've already put the tires on the car. If you don't take my money, then what the hell do you propose—"

"She gave you permission to use her card?"

"*Yes,* of course," I said. "It's not a very big deal."

He made a face as if he was doing something terrifically illegal or something, like he was doing me a giant favor by letting me use my mom's credit card. He finally rang me up, but not before being a pain in my ass. Anyway, after I signed the bill, my mom and I walked to the parking lot and picked up the car—four new Michelins planted beneath us.

Pulling up to Carlin Park sometime in the early evening, with the Florida sun preparing to set—the sky full of purples and blues and oranges, the most beautiful colors you've ever seen in your life, the type of colors that make you feel like the sky looks like that *everywhere,* the type of colors that make you feel like you're in the middle of absolutely nowhere, and like even if the entire world blew up in some giant mushroom cloud you wouldn't even know about it—my mom and I sat quietly. We made a right at the entrance to the park and didn't say a word as the car slowly crunched along the gravel road and came to a stop alongside the pond. It was so quiet you could hardly whisper without feeling like you were screaming.

"Hey, Ma?" I said very quietly.

She sort of grunted.

"I'm glad you're here with me, Mom."

She had her head leaned back against the headrest with a relaxed but childlike smile on her face. The way she was sitting there with that smile sort of reminded me of this one particular time a few years ago when we were in St. Augustine. It was sometime in December, right around the solstice. We'd left New York at four that morning, I remember, and we'd been on the road for close to eighteen hours by the time we got too tired to keep going. We stopped in St. Augustine and took a hotel room in some lavish joint called the Microtel. There were two beds in the room, and I took the one closest to the john. I don't remember what time it was, but it was the middle of the night, and I started to get pretty restless. So to entertain myself a little I started jumping on my bed. First I would back up to the door, get a running start, and then jump as high as I could and do a belly flop onto the bed. My mom was so weak and exhausted she could hardly move an inch, and the bandage around her waist was bothering her something awful. I forgot to mention that. She'd just gotten out of the hospital about two days before we'd left for Florida. She had needed a few transfusions and things to keep her blood count stable, and they'd kept her in the hospital for five days. She was still pretty anemic by the time we got to St. Augustine. Anyway, I kept doing that business of getting a running start and diving onto my bed. But after about the tenth time, I stopped and just lay there watching my mom rest with her eyes closed. I remember feeling so terrible I almost wished I were dead. I remember feeling guilty that I was able to run and jump and all my mom could do was rest. I got so depressed all of a sudden. I got so depressed that I put my face between the sheets on the bed and started to cry. I was trying to be subtle about it and not make any noise. But what happened was, all of a sudden, I heard these loud footsteps, sort of like somebody was *running* inside our room. I looked up and saw my mom running toward her bed—sort of an awkward walk-run, but a run just the same. And then, you wouldn't believe it if you saw it, but she dove head-first right into all the blankets and pillows on her bed. It wasn't a *full* dive, of course, but a sort of half dive, an awkward, *adorable* dive. My eyes were all watery, and I could hardly see her when she looked up, but I could make out the big childlike smile on her face. I could also tell she was trying to pretend she hadn't just used every last ounce of strength in her body to make that dive.

"*Ma,*" I said, and wiped my eyes quickly. "What the hell are you doing? You're going to hurt your—"

"Take it easy, boy," she said and let herself fall on her side, keeping that big childlike smile on her face. "There's nothing wrong with aiming high for those bandanas and October supplies."

I kept my eyes closed and thought about that while my mom and I sat in the car at Carlin Park. It was so quiet you could hardly hear anything except the ducks quacking, and every few seconds you'd hear something splash into the water. I let my head fall to the side and rest against my window. I kept my eyes closed and just thought about things for a few minutes.

I looked over at my mom and saw that she still had her eyes closed. I could see them through her sunglasses.

"Mama," I said. "I kept meaning to tell you—I mean, I know you probably don't like to talk about it, and I don't either, but that time, Ma, that we were in the Franklin Medical—"

"*I want to feel high like I did back then when time passed slowly, and a friend was still a friend . . .*" she started singing softly.

"I know this song, Ma. This is the Jennie DeVoe song from the—"

"*And I want you to be just what you said you'd be to me, always right beside me 'til the very end, and I want to paint skies, I want to leave time, feel with my hands, let my eyes be blind.*"

"I can see you sitting on that bench right outside FAO Schwarz and singing that song to yourself clear as day, Ma, as clear as fleece and blue suede shoes. I swear to everything decent and holy I can."

She kept on humming to herself, not singing any more words, but just humming—the sort of humming you do when you don't know the words to a song, you just know the melody.

"Sun will be knocking off work for the day soon," I said

and looked up toward the sky. "Sorry you didn't get to see those flying fish, Ma."

She stopped humming and sort of cleared her throat.

"I saw," she said.

"What, the fish?"

"I saw them."

"When, Ma?"

She cleared her throat again, but when she spoke, her voice sounded like a fifteen-year-old girl's.

"Before, when you were resting. I saw."

I paused and looked out my window.

"You mean when I was—"

"Never saw anything so gorgeous in my life—like silver dollars coming out of the water," she said slowly and softly, letting her head lean back against the headrest and turn to the side, facing her window. "*And I want you to be just what you said you'd be to me, always right beside me 'til the very end*—" she sang slowly.

I looked over at the pond. It was still. "Then they're still there," I whispered.

Sunday Way

N ext to winter, the summer is my least favorite time to be in New York City. You always hear people telling you about how terrific it is and everything, but that's purely for the uninitiated. The city is too congested and crowded and smoldering to be anything but hell on earth during the summer. The subways are around ten thousand degrees, and the highways are more packed with cars than a goddamn airport parking lot. There's nowhere to go and nothing nice to see. There's construction everywhere and the parks are filthy. Summer is, hands down, my second-least favorite time to be in the city, and especially to be in the backseat of a smelly beige Buick. I always get nauseous when I'm in the backseat of a cab.

"Whath wrong, honey? You feeling all right?" the cab

driver asked me. I had my head leaning against the window.

"Fine," I said. "I'm fine."

I didn't feel fine, though. That goddamn Buick stank like the worst pile of brown trout that I'd ever encountered. It was also hot as an atomic bomb.

"You eat breakfatht thith morning, honey?"

I always get stuck with a whackadoo for a cab driver. I swear to God I do. That's why I hardly ever take cabs. You should've seen *this* one, though. She really took the cake. She had one of these very raspy, smoked-out voices, a hacking, phlegm-filled cough, and a lisp that was thicker than her glasses. But not just that—she was *old*. Old for a cab driver, that is. She had these really big, thick glasses, and a mane that practically reached the roof of the god-damn car. She looked pretty beaten up, too. She had that *divorced* look. She looked like she'd been divorced ten times and been to a lot of different courts. From where I was sitting I could only see her profile, but she looked pretty divorced from the side.

I glanced over at my mom, who was sitting in the back-seat with me, just behind the driver. My mom looked as nauseous as I felt. It's hard *not* to feel nauseous when you're the passenger in a car driving in New York. Every place you go is so disgustingly crowded and congested, and everything around you is so ugly and depressing—from the people to all the goddamn construction everywhere.

"We'll be there soon, Ma," I said very softly. She had her sunglasses on, but I could tell she heard me.

"I'm thorry, honey?" the cab driver said. She sure liked to say the word *honey* a lot.

"Yeah, I ate breakfast this morning," I said and sort of took a deep breath. "I always get sick when I'm in the backseat. Reminds me of the goddamn school bus."

We were stuck in traffic on Jewel Avenue, right around the area where I went to high school. We'd missed the same stoplight three times already and were on our way to missing it a fourth. That's one thing about New York—you can sit at the same traffic light for twenty minutes sometimes. The cab driver was looking at a crossword puzzle while we sat there. She'd been working on that thing since my mom and I had gotten in the car. Every chance she got to look at it, she did. Even in slow traffic.

"Doeth Washington have a capital, honey?" she asked me. Jesus, she sounded like she'd been smoking ten packs a day for the last fifty years, and that lisp was driving me crazy.

"Well, actually, Wash—"

"Honey, which courthouth are we going to on Queenth Boulevard? There're a few of them, you know."

"The criminal courthouse. The one all the way down Queens Boulevard."

"You in thome kind of trouble, honey?"

"Yeah, a little bit," I said.

I was due in criminal court that morning on account of some pretty serious trouble I'd gotten myself into back in April. It's kind of a convoluted story, and I don't much feel like getting into it. Anyway, I guess the cab driver had lost interest in knowing what the capital of Washington was.

"And *that'th* what you're *wearing?*" she asked in a very

hyperactive way. "Honey, you might want to go back and put thomething a little nither on, maybe thomething that hath thome colorth in it." Jesus, that woman was loud. And a real nosey parker, too.

I laughed her off. "I'm all right, ace," I said. "Besides, I'll be honest with you. If they're going to throw the book at me they're going to throw the book at me no matter *what* the hell I'm wearing. That's how they are in this city. They rip you off six ways until sundown."

"Honey, I don't want to get into political thingth with you, I jutht thaid you might want to wear thomething that ithn't all black. I mean, let'th not get into anything ludicrouth here, you know what I'm thaying, honey?"

Now do you see why I hardly ever take a cab? Some of these people are out of their minds, I'm telling you. I guess that's what sitting on your ass in traffic all day will do to you. Anyway, I just sort of gave her a laugh and didn't make an issue out of it.

Mostly, I felt bad for my mom sitting in that car. She had her head leaning back against the headrest, and her mouth was open as if she were out of breath—she looked sick as a parrot. I was glad she was there with me, though. I'd never been to criminal court before, and because of the seriousness of the charge against me, I didn't really feel like going by myself.

I reached out and grabbed her hand, and she turned her head to the side slowly and looked at me with her dark sunglasses on. I could see her eyes *slightly,* though.

I whispered to her so the nosey driver wouldn't hear me. "We'll be gone soon, Ma, okay? We're going to get out of here forever, I promise you. Let's just stick it out today, and after that we'll slip out. One more day. Just be strong today, and then I'll get us out of here."

My mom smiled at me. Her teeth looked like they had a black outline around them, like her mouth was dry as a bone, like she hadn't had a drink of water in a year. I squeezed her hand a few times and then let go.

Traffic was bad on Jewel Avenue, as usual, so to occupy my time I went ahead and started reading some dirty magazine that was on the floor in the back of the cab. It was one of these hotshot New York magazines, the *New Yorker* or some other elitist rag like that. Typical silver watch magazine—the kind that non–New York New Yorkers subscribe to, the kind that non–New York New Yorkers work for, the kind that prints bits and bats of a book and then does a critique of each piece, and then does an interview with the writer at the end.

I was reading this one story that was lifted from a novel written by some young big-shot writer. It was about this boy who's just moved out to the sticks with his family. He doesn't have any friends or anything, and the nearest neighbors are about two miles away. The only friend he has is his dog, Lindsay, and all they do over summer vacation is sit behind their house by this very large pond that has goldfish in it. His mother is up the creek in bad health and stays in bed all day, and his father is sort of a lounge lizard, sort of an absentee father, but every once in a while he joins them by the pond and shoots the breeze with his son. The father keeps telling him about how the pond is slowly drying up because it hasn't been raining all that much, and how the fish are going to die if the water gets any more shallow. So what the boy does, is every day he fills up a cup with water from the kitchen sink, runs out back, and pours it into the pond, hoping to keep it filled up. He does this about a thousand times a day for the entire summer.

To be honest with you, I was getting a real charge out of reading it. I mean, for a story in the *New Yorker*, it was pretty damn good, even though, like every big-shot story, it paid *way* too much attention to detail. For instance, in the scene where the boy pours his first cup of water into the pond, he reaches into his back pocket and takes out a penny so he can make a wish to God that the pond will never go dry and the fish won't suffocate. Only the way it was written, it takes about three pages for the little bastard to even get the penny out of his *pocket*. And then, after he *does* get it out of his pocket, the penny is described to death, even down to what year penny it is. That kind of thing can drive me out of my box. Personally, I think it's a pretty cheap parlor trick. It seems to me, a lot of these big-money hotshot writers have very little to say for themselves, and to make it *appear* like they have a lot more to say than they actually do, they make their books a lot more wordy than they need to be. They probably sit at their typewriters with a goddamn thesaurus next to them. That alone can ruin a book for me. Frankly, I'd prefer a book that takes an hour to read rather than one that takes two weeks to read and does nothing but bang on about what year a penny in a boy's pocket was made.

Anyway, after I got done reading, I put the magazine back down on the floor where I'd found it.

"You read that thtory about the family that hath the goldfish pond, honey?" She was looking at me through the rearview mirror.

"Yeah," I said. "Just finished as a matter of—"

"Ithn't it *amathing?* They're thaying it'th like another *Huckleberry Finn.*"

I got a kick out of that one. The only thing this story had in common with *Huckleberry Finn* is that it had a body of water in it.

"Yeah, I can definitely see the comparison," I said to

her. With some people, you really can't tell them a story isn't like another story. Some people aren't even worth straightening out because they're too dead from the neck up. If I'd have told her that the only reason the *New Yorker* was comparing this story to *Huckleberry Finn* was because magazines are too simple and too toilet-trained to resist making comparisons to older stories, that they're too attached to standard procedure to just let a good story stand on its own legs, to just let it be its own story and let the audience decide what they think it should be compared to, if anything, then she probably would've told me that I was wrong and too critical of the *New Yorker* and other big-shot magazines. So I didn't waste my time.

We didn't do too much talking the rest of the ride. It was too hot in the car, and I was too nauseous to feel like saying anything.

"You awake back there, honey?" the cab driver asked me when we got to the courthouse.

"Yeah," I said. "You can just drop me on the corner here and I'll walk across the street."

"You sure, honey?"

"Yeah, it's fine. I could use the exercise." I looked over at my mom and kind of gave her a laugh.

The driver pulled the car over in front of some god-damn parking facility. While I was getting some money out of my pocket, she picked up her crossword puzzle and started working on it.

"Did you know that Thaddam Huthein hath thome type of thkin canther?" It was a very funny thing to say.

"No, I didn't, ace," I said and let out a little laugh.

"Well he doeth. He'th a very thick man. He doethn't have very long to live. Couldn't have happened to a nither man, huh?"

I just sort of gave her another laugh. I didn't really feel like getting into any kind of discussion with her. You really have to be careful with some of these cabbies. Once you get into a discussion with them, they'll chew on until they're blue in the face. I guess they're lonely or something, being in a cab all day by themselves.

Anyway, then she turned around completely and looked

at me. Boy, was she a sight to see. She had all of three teeth in her mouth, which would explain her lisp, and there were gray whiskers sticking out of her goddamn chin. She was certainly a sight.

"Good luck in court, honey," she said. I thanked her and gave her a ten-spot as I got out of the car. After my mom and I had crossed the street and were standing in front of the courthouse, I turned around to see if she'd driven away. She hadn't. She was still sitting there working on that crossword puzzle.

I'd never been to a criminal courthouse before, but it didn't come as any surprise that out in front of the place was a line about two miles long. Every single piece of human excrement and his brother was due in court that morning, it seemed, and the place looked more like the goddamn Bronx Zoo than a courthouse. I was immediately sorry that I'd even shown up, and I felt even *more* lousy that my mom had to see me surrounded by that filth. It made me feel awful.

I was told to be there at nine, but on account of the

line I didn't wind up getting inside until nine-thirty. My mom and I took seats in the back of the court and waited until the judge finally got there and started hearing the cases, most of which were assault and drug related.

We sat there for over an hour and they still hadn't gotten around to me yet. My mom was sitting there with her sunglasses on.

"Do you believe this?" I asked her. She shook her head and adjusted her glasses. "I'm sorry you have to see me in this place, Ma," I whispered. "Maybe we ought to leave straight from here, shoot straight up to Lake George regardless of what they decide to do with me. How about that? We'll leave and won't ever come back, not even for our stuff."

My mom was looking at me through her sunglasses, and she sort of dropped her head a little and, with a tired expression on her face, whispered, "I don't want maggots all over my face, Mike."

"I know, Mama. I know you don't. But I'm going to take you out of here. We'll find a real quiet road that's in the middle of nowhere, a road—"

"Stop *talking!*" I heard some hotshot cop yell at me. He was standing in the back of the courtroom with his arms crossed, and the son of a bitch yelled so loudly I damn near had a coronary. I gave him a look but didn't say anything. I was in enough trouble as it was.

I gave my mom a pat on the thigh and then didn't say anything else. My nerves were shot to hell anyway, and like I always do when I'm nervous, I was cutting the cheese left and right.

Eventually, after all the armed robbery and drug-related cases, they got to me. I heard some woman—and I use the word very loosely—call out my name.

"*The next case will be the City of New York versus M. Dylan Raskin.*"

I gave my mom a nod and then made my way up to the front of the room, where the judge was sitting on his throne. I'd practically signed my pants by the time I got up there.

The judge was a very old bastard, and he was busy sorting through papers while I stood there like a schmuck.

Before he said anything to me, I heard that guy-guy cop in the back of the room yell at someone for talking too loudly. I tried not to laugh, but it was impossible. These idiot cops are always telling people not to talk.

"Something funny, mister?" the judge asked me in a very sarcastic way.

"No, sir," I said.

"Because I wouldn't be laughing quite so industriously if I were standing where you are right now."

"Well I apologize, ace," I said.

Right away, he started looking at me very seriously and everything. Then he looked over at that woman who'd called out my name at the start of the case, then back at me again.

"Look, mister. This is a courtroom, not a playground. I'm the judge, and you will refer to me as *Your Honor* or *sir*. Do I make myself clear?" He certainly was one miserable son of a bitch.

"I got it," I said.

He went back to flipping through his papers.

"Okay," the prune-faced judge finally said, "this is the City of New York versus M. Dylan Raskin, a.k.a. Michael D. Raskin." He stopped to cough. "The charge being riding a bicycle on the sidewalk." He put his fist to his mouth and cleared his throat.

"Your Honor," I said. "There weren't any signs anywhere saying that I couldn't ride my—"

"Look, mister, I wasn't there, so don't tell me what there was and what there wasn't. The fine will be fifty dollars," he said very nonchalantly.

"*Fifty* dollars?" I said. "Judge, I've been riding my bike on the same street since I was a kid. Since when is it a crime to ride your bicycle on the—"

"You just *said* it, Mr. Raskin. It *is* a crime, and perhaps if you paid more attention to the laws of the city you live in you'd know this."

"Well I won't be living in this city for very much longer," I sort of mumbled. "And neither will the rest of you."

The judge put his glasses on and moved some paperwork around.

"Excuse me, Mr. Raskin?"

"I believe that it's only a matter of time, Your Honor, before a nuclear device explodes in this city and kills millions of people. And if you don't believe—"

"You've got some smart mouth, young man," he said. He took his glasses off and started looking at me as if he might jump over the bench and strangle me. "I won't allow you to say those kinds of things in this court. Am I making myself clear? What a *horrible* thing to say. Just *horrible*."

"Your Honor, you might not like to think about it— *nobody* does—but I believe it's coming. That's why my mom and I are getting out of here. We're not sticking around for—"

"Son, I'd ordinarily feel compelled to educate you in the ways of the world, but I'm not going to waste either your time or mine." He put his glasses back on and coughed again. While he was thinking of what to say next, I turned around quickly to check on my mom. She was still sitting where she was before, still with her sunglasses on, and her head leaned back. The way she was sitting there with her head back reminded me of that time in Lake George when she was sitting on the park bench whispering the "I shall not die" prayer. I kept wondering, while I was standing up there before the judge, if she was reciting the prayer while she sat there in the court. And although I knew she wouldn't be able to see, I mouthed the words "yellow eyes no more" at her.

Meanwhile, I could hear the grumpy old judge mumbling to himself, trying to think of what to say as he flipped through some papers.

"Here's something fascinating in front of me," he finally said and adjusted his glasses. He was looking at a piece of paper. "You've been having quite a year, haven't you, Mr. Raskin? Let's see, writing rubber checks against an account in the name of a deceased person, using that same deceased person's credit card, and being a wise guy to the officer who cited you for irresponsibly riding your bicycle on the sidewalk at the intersection of Jewel Avenue and Kissena Boulevard." He started doing this annoying chuckle that teachers and cops made famous. "Listen to this, Yolanda," he said to that dirty bitch who'd called out my name at the start of the case. "This is what Smart Mouth here said to the citing officers when they ticketed him for riding his bicycle on the sidewalk. Officer Toast of the 107th Precinct wrote it down. Quote: 'You're hoodwinking me. Airplanes fly into buildings in this city, we're under the threat of a nuclear terrorist attack in Manhattan, Nazi Geico charges four hundred dollars each month to insure a car, gas prices are two dollars a gallon and it all gets wasted sitting in gridlock traffic, and you're ticketing me for riding my bike on Jewel Avenue. Where the hell am I—Tehran?'"

After he finished reading it, the both of them started cracking up together, and ole prune-face took his glasses off. They were enjoying the hell out of themselves, apparently.

"You're a real prophet of doom, young man," he said to me. "You're lucky you didn't get yourself arrested at the scene." He started putting all his papers together to show me that he was ready to move on to the next case. He also put his glasses back on, which I got a real charge out of. Bastards like him have only two expressions—glasses on and glasses off. "Pay your fine and have a nice life wherever you go, Mr. Raskin. Next ca—"

"This is *ridiculous!*" I yelled out. "I mean, this is really ridiculous, Your Honor. The damn economy's in the dumps, nobody has any money, the country's at war, and you're ex*torting* money from me. You're actually *stealing*—"

"*Sir!*" that bigmouth cop in the back of the room yelled at me. "Leave the room right now." I turned around and saw that he was making his way to the front of the court.

All of a sudden, I felt like I was going to have a stroke.

"What the hell is *wrong* with all of you people?" I screamed. "All of you crazy people who live in this city— you're all being set up! You're all being set up for a nuclear holocaust. Don't you realize that? It's *coming* and you'd better wake up and stop giving a damn about meaningless things like bicycles on the sidewalk and—"

"*Get him out of here right now,*" the grumpy old judge yelled out to the guy-guy cop.

"Throw me out. I don't care. I'm getting out of this cockroach city anyway, me and my mom. We're both going to get far, far away from this horrible—"

Just as I was saying all that, I felt that guy-guy cop come up from behind me and grab my arm. He was trying to show how much of a big shot he was by squeezing my arm like he was going to break it.

"This way, sir," he said as he pulled me by the arm. Real big shot. He only outweighed me by three hundred pounds, that monkey.

"I can *walk*, for God's sake," I said and yanked my arm away. He grabbed my arm again and kept pulling at me. "I wouldn't do that if I were you," I said as he dragged me out of the room. "I've got people watching over me, man, and you'd better—"

"Another word out of you and I'm going to place you under arrest," he said like a real tough guy. It was so obvious he was trying to make his voice sound deeper than it actually was. Goddamn guy-guys.

"Yeah, whatever you say, Robocop," I said. I was halfway

expecting him to arrest me right then and there, but luckily he just told me to pay my fine—to avoid having a warrant put out on me—and leave. Then he walked back into the courtroom while fixing up his red pompadour. My tongue was so numb I kept feeling like I was going to have a stroke, and the back of my shirt was soaking wet from sweating so damn much.

The *last* thing in the world I needed was to have a warrant put out on me—I had enough problems—so I went over to the clerk to pay my stupid fine. She was a big old black woman sitting behind a sheet of Plexiglas.

"Here to pay my fine, ma'am," I said.

"You was the guy on the bicycle?"

"Yes, I was. Judge said the fine was twenty bucks." I figured I'd be economical with the truth and maybe save myself a few dollars. I shouldn't have had to pay anything at *all*, frankly.

"He said fitty, not twenty."

She had the ticket sitting right there on the desk, so there was no way I could argue the toss with her. I shot her a quick laugh. "Well, you can't blame a guy for trying, right?"

She didn't answer me.

"How you gonna pay for that?" she finally asked.

Obviously, I didn't have fifty bucks in cash on me. I probably had *five,* if I was lucky. I'd spent the rest of my money on the cab ride.

"Credit card, I guess." I slid my card through the slot.

"This your card? Who's Franken Raskin?"

"It's my mother's card, *Francine* Raskin. I'll owe her back for it."

She didn't answer me again. She just went ahead and rang everything up. I was worried for a minute that the credit card was going to decline. The goddamn receipt didn't print for about two minutes. While I was waiting for it, I kept getting this pain in my chest—sort of like a sharp, stabbing pain right around my heart. It sort of scared me for a minute, to be honest with you.

Anyway, when the receipt finally printed, I signed it and then got ready to look for my mom so that we could get the hell out of there.

"Stay off your bike," the clerk said to me as I was walking away.

I didn't answer her. Instead, I just stayed in the lobby and looked around for my mom. My goddamn chest was killing me. Luckily, I didn't have to wait around too long for her. She came walking out after just a few minutes, and we were able to get the hell out of there.

Queens Boulevard was crowded when we walked outside. It's always crowded around there, mostly with taxis, gypsy cabs, buses, and businesspeople. My mind was racing so much, though, that I didn't even think about hailing a cab or catching a bus. I probably didn't have enough money on me anyway. I *know* I didn't, actually.

"Looks like we're walking, Ma. Looks like we're walking back to Sixty-eighth Drive. It's good exercise anyway, you know? Besides, I don't feel too well, Ma. I'm not well, Mama. Please help me, for the love of God, please help me, Ma," I was saying as we slowly walked away from the courthouse and down Queens Boulevard. I had this horrible feeling in my chest, sort of like if I took too deep a breath, my heart was going to attack me. And I couldn't stop my hands from shaking. They were shaking like they shake when I'm cold, or when I'm nervous.

I reached over and grabbed my mom's shoulder. My chest was hurting so much I could hardly talk straight.

"Going to be away from here soon, Ma, okay? Just give me a minute to catch my breath—wait—then we'll get moving again. Just got to keep our strength, Ma." My chest hurt so bad I could hardly breathe. I kept trying to take a deep breath, hoping that maybe the pain would go away, but it never did. "God, I can't hardly get my breath, Ma. Wait, let's stop here, just for a quick minute, let's just stand here, right against this building." We were standing in front of a bank, and I leaned up against the building and tried to catch my breath. "I'm going to get us out of here, Mom. I don't want you to worry. I'm going to get us away. You don't have to worry about any—" I kept trying to catch my wind. "We'll go to Lake George, right near—"

"Mike, please don't do this to your—"

"*No*, don't—please don't strain yourself, Ma. It kills me when I—" I was practically hyperventilating.

"You have to let me go," my mom said.

"What're you *talking* about, Ma?" I sounded like someone having an asthma attack. "I'm not letting *anyone* go—I'm taking you with me, just like I promised you I would. God, my chest. God*damn* it. My chest is killing me. You remember when we were trying to think of where we could go, where we could hide out? I know where it is." I was looking up toward the sky, still trying to catch my breath, and still leaning up against that bank. "Just off Route 9, just outside the Lake George village, past Rosie's Diner, just beyond the entrance to the thruway, past Grandma's Back Porch Restaurant. We'll go to that little private road we like, the one that's always covered in dead leaves no matter what month it is, the road that cracks and pops when you drive on it, the one that looks like you can sit down in the middle of it and close your eyes and never have to worry about a car coming and running you over, the one you once swore to the moon and stars was land's end, the last of all October side streets, the only Sunday safe spot left on this godforsaken earth. I don't know what that road is called, but we'll rename it *Sunday*. Sunday something. Sunday—"

"*Way*. Sunday Way," my mom said, while her floppy blondish hair got tossed off her forehead by the wind.

"Yeah," I said. "Sunday Way." I kept trying to gasp for air, even though it hurt my chest like hell. "I won't let the maggots get to your face on Sunday Way. What I'll do is every time they get too close to you, I'll go and grab my lucky blue bandana and quickly wrap it around your face to keep them out. But what we've got to do, Ma, is we've got to get our strength back—both of us. I'll catch my breath, you'll catch your breath, and then we'll start walking again. We just have to get our strength back, okay? That's all we've got to do, and the rest will be downhill. I know it will be."

"I don't want you to miss me, Mike. Not so much that you can't—"

"*No*, you don't have to say it, Ma. *Jesus*, I can't breathe. I can't—"

I was so out of breath that I just sat down right on the

sidewalk, right next to the bank, with my back still leaned up against the building. I didn't have enough wind left in me to talk anymore. My chest hurt too much from trying to take deep breaths, so I just sat there and concentrated on my breathing. One quick breath in, then a short one out. One quick breath in, then a short one out. I kept my head leaned back against the building.

My mom walked over and stood in front of me.

"My little Sunday Way boy," she said and put her hand on my head. "Always the sweetest little Sunday Way boy . . . I'll come with you to Lake George."

I was too out of breath to answer. The sky looked like it was spinning.

"Mike?"

I was hardly able to get out a whisper.

"*Mike,* are you—"

"I'm going to be okay, Mom," I said. "Don't worry, Mama."

I don't know how long we stayed there by that bank, but it was a good while. Even though there were a lot of cars and a lot of people around, we didn't bother to move. We didn't even talk. I sat there, and she stood over me, keeping an eye on me, making sure I could breathe, making sure I was all right.

For my life, I couldn't tell you how long it was, but after some time I started to feel a little better—when I got my breath back, that is, and was able to stand up. My goddamn back was killing me from leaning against that building for so long. When I first stood up I got so dizzy that I almost fell over and popped my clogs.

"Okay, let's go home," I said and shook off my shirt. "It's only a couple of miles. Not sure I'll be able to keep up with you, Ma, but I'll try my best."

My mom was standing in front of me, her dark sunglasses still on her face, her short hair being tossed around, and her shirt collar reaching up to her chin every time the wind blew.

"I bet this makes walking a lot easier," I said jokingly, patting her on the back. "If I had a shirt collar like this one, there's no telling what I could do. Anyway, I'll try and use my youth to my advantage, but I don't think I'll be able to keep up with you, Mama. Don't worry about me, though. I'll be right behind you. I'll be right behind you the whole time, Ma. You lead and I'll follow. That's how we'll get home. But I'll tell you something, Franny, if it's the *last* thing I do, I swear to everything sacred and holy, I won't hear anymore of this business about missing you. You and I are golden eggs—we don't belong here in the first place, neither one of us. And we're not coming back—not this time, not *any* time. There're a million places we could go, Ma—a *million* places—and our only limit is our goddamn sanity."

Yellow Eyes No More

I can still remember how the door to our room in the Franklin Hospital Medical Center was outlined in light. It was dark inside our room, even though it was noontime, but the hallway lights outside our door seeped in just enough to create a sort of ash-gray lighting. One thing about ash-gray lighting—it can sure make you feel like you're dying, even when you're not dying, even when you *know* you're not, even when they *assure* you, by every bible and prayer, you're not dying.

My mom's feet were sticking out of the red fleece blanket that was covering her, and her little white and pink socks didn't exactly look warm. So I took one of the sheets off the table next to the bed and covered her bottom half with it. Even though it was the back end of summertime, it was cold as hell in our room. About three weeks earlier, I'd gotten myself a gray, fleece-lined work jacket from a store on Parsons Boulevard. It was thirty-five bucks, and I'd determined that it was the only jacket I'd ever need in my entire life. It wasn't *nice* or anything—it was ugly as sin— but it was the sort of jacket you could see yourself in while you were lying low after a nuclear war, after most of the world was dead, after there was no place left to go, when it was cold and desolate out and you were sick as a goddamn parrot, sick from radiation poisoning and starvation and nuclear winter, and you were sleeping in a foxhole with a fire next to you waiting to die. But it was *also* the sort of jacket you could see yourself wearing in late October, right around Halloweentime, walking through a small fishing village like Southport, North Carolina, where no one knows you, where you're so anonymous you practically don't exist, where you're practically in*vis*ible. It was an October sort of jacket. Even in September, it was an October sort of jacket. That's why I was glad I had it with me when my mom and I were cooped up in that cold goddamn hospital room. I hadn't taken it off once since we'd been there.

"Mom?" I said. I didn't expect a reply. She was so tired and weak by that time, I didn't expect her to even be able to open up her eyes. They'd been shut for nearly three days. The only times she opened them were when one of the goddamn nurses came in to ask whether we were sleeping.

Anyway, I called her again, but she didn't answer. She just lay there. Breathing. I reached over and made sure her blankets were tucked in around her.

"Just like you used to tuck me in, Ma," I said quietly. "Looks like this Lake George fleece blanket came in handy, huh? If only Jacksonville could see us now." I unzipped my October jacket and let it open, then ran my hand over my buzzed head. "I'm so sorry I let you down, Mom. I mean, I know I promised you we'd be off to the races by now—I promised you that and, God love you, I failed, and now we're stuck in this goddamn ash-gray, frostbitten place. This is the *last* place on earth I ever wanted us to be, Ma, the *last* place, and if I had the strength and you were feeling better, I'd hoist you over my goddamn shoulder—fleece blankets and all—and carry you out to the car and get us the hell out of here. You *have* to believe that's what I'd do, Ma. Because lying around in this place, this *can't* be our purpose, Ma. I won't hear it and I won't believe it, damn it, that our purpose is to sit around this drafty ole hospital room waiting for the next plate of watermelon and ginger ale and getting asked thirty questions by some idiotic nurse whose idea of a good time is cleaning up manure out of a goddamn bedpan. I don't care so much about me, but *you*, Mama, *you* don't deserve this, and I swear to you this isn't your purpose, and I'm not going to let it end like this. I won't let you go like this, Ma. I can't and I won't—"

I got cut off by some pain in my ass knocking on the door. There was *always* some pain in the ass knocking on the door in that place. Ten million times a day. Even at night. At night they'd knock on the door and wake you up to ask whether or not you were sleeping. They'd actually *ask* you if you were sleeping. And if you didn't answer, they'd ask *again*, only louder. I don't understand hospital people. They go to school for fifty years, and they wind up waking you up by *asking* whether or not you're sleeping. It just doesn't make any goddamn sense to me. I'm starting to think the more years you spend in school, the dumber you end up.

Before I even had a chance to ask who it was, to say stay the hell out because my mom was sleeping, the door opened. That's another thing that hospital people always do. They always knock but don't wait for an answer.

"Mr. *Radskin?*" I heard some incompetent moron yell out. I purposely didn't answer her. She came walking in anyway. I knew she would. When she saw me, I quickly put my finger over my mouth and said *shhhh,* then sort of tilted my head toward my mom so old Wonder Nurse would see that she was sleeping.

"You *hungry?*" she asked. None too friendly, either. She obviously had some hell of a winning personality. She was a large black woman, and she was standing there with some greasy brown bag in one hand. Her other hand was on her goddamn hip. I hadn't seen her before.

"Not particularly," I said. "What the hell is it anyway?"

"I just deliver the food, I don't inspect it," she said.

"Well then why don't you just go ahead and leave it on the table. *I'll* inspect it later and maybe one of us will eat it." I adjusted my October jacket so that the sleeves didn't cover part of my hands. I also noticed that the name tag on her shirt said *Cleopatra Thomas* on it. I'm not making this up. That's *actually* what her name tag said. The goddamn Queen of Egypt works at the Franklin Hospital Medical Center. Who'd have known?

"Pardon?" she said. She was giving me this very impatient, hostile look, and that bag of grease she was holding was starting to stink up the entire room.

"I *said* I'm an IAEA inspector and will *personally* inspect that bag of grease myself if you leave it on the goddamn table next to the phone." I couldn't help myself. I didn't expect her to blow her top because of it, though.

All of a sudden, she just sort of tossed the grease bag on the floor and put both her hands on her hips.

"Why you giving me attitude for? If you don't want that food—"

"*Hey,*" I interrupted. "You want to keep it down, for God's sake?" That ten-ton piece of sludge didn't even care that my mom and I were trying to get some rest, that we both felt like crap, that we'd both been sitting around in that hellhole for days freezing our asses off and being woken up every ten minutes.

"Don't tell me to take it easy. Stop giving me attitude or I'm a forget I work here. You know what I'm sayin'?"

You should've seen the look on this beast. She looked like she was rabid, for God's sake. Some professional. Some goddamn professional.

"All right," I said. "I lied about being an IAEA inspector. I'm currently unemployed and just staying in the hospital taking care of my sick mom." I looked over at where my mom was lying. "She's got dyspraxia and can't talk anymore. But listen, if you get us out of here before a nuclear bomb explodes in New York, I'll eat that whole goddamn bag of grease right in front of you, I swear to God. And I'm a vege*ta*rian."

You should've *seen* the look on the Queen of Egypt's

face. She looked like she was about to go completely ape. Luckily for me, she didn't say anything else, though. All she wound up doing was giving the bag of grease a kick and then walked out mumbling to herself about how she hated her stupid job. I was relieved to see her leave, believe me. She had a face that was like the back end of a bus, and I couldn't stand to look at her for another second. I bet the *real* Queen of Egypt, the *real* Cleopatra from thousands of years ago, looks better than her *now*. I can't stand these useless jerk-offs who hate their jobs and take their misery out on other people. In my opinion, if you hate your job so much, you ought to just go out and get another one.

Anyway, after Cleopatra went back to her tomb, I let the sleeves of my October jacket drop and cover the tops of my hands again. I liked it better that way. Primarily because my hands are always so damn cold. Even during the summertime, sometimes, they're cold. I can be at the beach and still have cold hands. I guess I'm just a thin-blooded son of a bitch.

My mom hadn't moved in two days, practically, and the

way she was breathing was starting to scare me. Each breath she took ended with a sort of grunt, a sort of *straining*. And her straining seemed to get more and more desperate by the minute. I sat up and watched her breathe in and out, her head tilted upward and her eyes closed, her face and neck unspeakably yellow.

"Hey, Mama?" I said and reached for her hand, my voice cracking something awful. Her hand was colder than mine. "I don't know if you can hear me, Mama, but I just want you to know that I'm right here, right beside you. I'm not going anywhere, Mom." I could hardly talk. I could hardly *hear* myself talking. I was practically whispering. Blanket fort whispering. "You're my strong, strong Mama, and you're going to be in Lake George soon. One way or another, okay? I'm here and I want you to let me do your worrying for you, Ma. You just concentrate on your breathing, all right? Just breathe, Ma. I know it hurts right now, I *know* it does, because God knows I can feel it. But if there's one thing I can promise you, if there's one thing I have on good goddamn authority, it's that it's not going to hurt like this forever, and I give you my word on that, Ma. I'm so incredibly s—"

I could feel my eyes starting to flood, so I wiped them with the sleeve of my October jacket. I couldn't bring myself to say another word because I thought I'd start to cry all over the goddamn place. So what I did instead was reach into my messenger bag on the table and pull out my portable CD player. It was a bright red one that my mom had received as a gift a few years ago. The only CD I had with me was a thunderstorm CD that I'd gotten in a nature store a few months back for my mom. Dr. Millani had told us that nature CDs were good for healing and soothing your nerves. She's very smart, Dr. Millani. Anyway, instead of putting the headphones in my ears, I just put them right down on my lap and let the thunderstorm CD play. It was loud enough that I could hear it without the headphones on. It reminded me of something that happened earlier in the year. It was right around April. I know it was right around April because we'd just gotten back from Florida, and we always went to Florida in April. My mom was at the North Shore University Hospital in the Don Monti building to get a blood transfusion. Only she wound up having a bad reaction to the transfusion, so they made her stay for a few days. I stayed there, too, and what I did was I set up two chairs so that they looked like a cot, and that's where I slept. The night before we left, I remember, I couldn't sleep worth a toss. I was too goddamn nervous. So, the whole entire night, practically, I sat up with my headphones on and just watched her sleep. But right around four in the morning, my mom woke up. I was surprised as all hell.

"Hey, Mama. Hey, honey," I said and ran my hand through her hair. I didn't bother to turn off the CD player. I just took the headphones out of my ears and let them fall around my neck, with the music still playing.

"What're you still doing up, Mike?" she asked.

"Nothing, Ma. Just looking around, thinking about things. Look, go back to sleep, will you? You feel all right?"

She nodded her head and said she felt okay. "What's that song you keep listening to?" she asked me. I wasn't sure what song she was talking about. I'd hardly been paying any attention to the music.

"I don't know," I said. "How does it go?"

She started humming the melody. Then she started singing, slowly and softly. "*I want to feel high like I did back then when time passed slowly, and a friend was still a friend, and I want you to be, just what you said you'd be to me, always right beside me, 'til the very end, and I want to paint skies, I want to leave time, feel with my hands, let my eyes be blind, you know when I hear your voice I've got no choice—*" She stopped to try and think of the rest of it.

"It's the new Jennie DeVoe song," I said. "It's called 'Don't It Sound Good.' You want to listen to it?"

She nodded her head.

I took the headphones off my neck and put them right on her bed, right near her right hand, and turned the song on. It was loud enough that both of us could hear it, even without having the headphones on.

"You going to be all right tonight, Ma?"

"*Yes,* for God's sake. Will you go back to sleep already?"

I could tell that she was so weak and tired she could hardly talk. She was trying hard not to show it, though. "Don't *worry* about me so much, Mike. I'm your mama and it's my job to worry about *you*. You know I'd never leave you, don't you? You're my little boy and you need your mama, even if you don't like to admit it. You think I'd ever leave you—my one and only son, my pride and joy, the apple in my eye— in this world by yourself? No way, man. I'll get my strength back, you'll see. So don't *worry* so much. Just try and get some rest. When we get out of here tomorrow, we'll pack our bags and go to Lake George for a couple of days, stay at the Super 8 and eat lots of good food. What do you say? I think we deserve it, don't you?"

"That sounds good to me, Ma. That sounds good to me," I said, my eyes starting to water.

"Good. Now shut up and let's listen to Jennie DeVoe," she said and closed her eyes.

I didn't bother to move the headphones or the portable CD player. I just let it sit there next to her right hand. The only thing I did was move one of the chairs closer to where my mom was and sat in it. I sat hunched over and rested my arms atop the safety railing on my mom's bed, and I lay my head down so that it was close to hers. She opened her eyes for a quick second and smiled but didn't say anything. I didn't say anything either. I just sat there in that dark hospital room with her while the music from the portable CD player played on the bed. I eventually fell asleep.

I kept thinking about that stuff while I sat there in that ash-gray hospital room listening to my mom's thunderstorm CD. It wasn't easy to hear because there was some old guy in one of the rooms across the hall screaming bloody murder. He wasn't even screaming about anything in particular—he was just screaming. Every ten seconds or so he'd just start screaming his goddamn lungs out. It was starting to give me the heebie-jeebies, to tell you the truth. I didn't make an issue out of it, though, because I didn't want to wake my mom or anything. So I just sat there in my October jacket and tried to listen to the thunderstorm CD and think about things.

You remember how I told you there was hardly a

minute that went by when there wasn't some pain in the ass knocking on the door? Well, I wasn't exaggerating. While I was sitting there keeping an eye on my mom and listening to my thunderstorm CD and thinking about everything, I heard the damn door open. This time, no one even *knocked*.

"*Hello?* Are we up in here?" I heard some loudmouth woman say.

"I am now," I said and turned off the CD player.

The woman closed the door behind her and then walked into the room like she owned the joint—very hurriedly and Friday afternoonish. She looked like she was in a mad rush to punch out for the weekend. She was one of these mousy older women who wears too much makeup and stinks like an old walk-in closet full of mothballs. In fact, the minute she walked in, the whole room immediately stank of mothballs. I felt like vomiting, to be honest with you.

She must've noticed that I was trying to get some rest because she started talking real low all of a sudden.

"Hello, Mr. Raskin," she said and sat down in a chair next to me. I was hoping she wouldn't sit so goddamn close. She really was stinking. Anyway, I didn't answer her. I was too busy holding my breath. Instead, I just smiled. "I didn't expect to see you back here. Do you remember me? We spoke the last time you were here with your mom."

"I remember you," I said. I *vaguely* did.

"Circumstances were very different last time, weren't they?" I didn't like the way she said that. She made it sound like the both of us were *dying*. I didn't like it one bit. I could also tell what she was setting me up for. She was setting me up for one of those goddamn inquisitions where they ask you all sorts of worthless questions to find out how the hell you're holding up. I also noticed her name tag said that in addition to being a nurse she was also a social worker and a chaplain. Her name was Margaret. If there's one thing these three-title people like to do, it's ask questions. I think they get pleasure out of it.

I tried to stop her from getting into a rhythm.

"What happened to the Queen of Egypt?" I asked her.

Right away she started looking at me like I was crazy.

"Who, sweetheart?"

"The Queen of Egypt. Cleopatra. She came in here before and threw my lunch on the floor."

"Oh, you mean Ms. Thomas." All of a sudden she knew who the hell I was talking about. "She's sort of ill-tempered, I'm sorry about that. She takes things around here very personally, maybe a little *too* personally. She thinks that when people say—oh, how should I say—sort of *quirky* things they're questioning—"

"Well I didn't say anything *quirky*. All I told her was that I'm sticking around in this dump with my mom until things get a little better, and all of a sudden she went completely bananas."

"Let's talk about that for a second."

"Fine. She took my lunch bag and tossed it on the floor and then went and gave it a—"

"No, no, I mean let's talk about what you said before. You said you're staying here until things get a little better." I didn't like the way she was looking at me when she said that. She was looking at me like she was a goddamn neurologist and I was about to go under the knife for some kind of brain surgery. She was looking at me with *sympathy,* with *pity.* I swear, all social workers are exactly the same. Every last one of them. "Do you think circumstances will get better any time soon?" she asked me.

I didn't answer her. I just kept looking over at my mom and thinking to myself that things probably *weren't* going to get any better anytime soon, and if they were, they were probably going to get worse first.

"Mr. Raskin?"

"I'm just not sure," I said.

"Mr. Raskin, I want to ask you a question, if I may." She wiped her beak with a tissue. And you should've *seen* the beak on her. She had a beak that would've certainly been the envy of many vultures. "Excuse me," she said, after she wiped her snot. Then she paused for a second and sort of looked over toward where my mom was lying. "Do you believe in God, Michael?"

It was funny. The way she asked me reminded me of

this one time a few years ago when my mom and I were in the clinic waiting to see Dr. Millani. It was in the falltime, I remember, and both of us were so nervous we could hardly keep our knees from shaking all over the place. I turned around in my seat and started looking out the window to try to settle my stomach, and all of a sudden, right out of left field, my mom kind of gave me a playful slap on the back.

"Hey," she said. She was smiling, but I could tell she was trying to conceal her nervousness. "Come here." She meant for me to lean over toward her.

"Can't you just tell me from there, Ma?"

"You think I want the whole world to know our business? C'mon, come *over* here. I want to tell you something."

"Ma, would you just—"

"If you don't come here *right* now, I swear on your father I'll walk out of here in a minute and you won't be able to stop me."

"For the love of *Christ* already, Ma, you ought to be on Broadway."

I turned around in my chair and leaned over toward her. I could see her foot tapping nervously on the floor. All of a sudden, she reached out and put her hand on the back of my head, as if she were about to tell me some big secret, and started whispering in my ear.

"What the hell are you—" I started to say.

"In Flanders Fields the poppies blow. Between the crosses row on row. That mark our place, and in the sky, the larks, still bravely singing, fly. Scarce heard amid the guns below." She paused for a second. "We are the—"

Before she could finish, one of the nurses yelled out her name, and she let go of me. We both took deep breaths and went in to see Dr. Millani.

The way Margaret asked me if I believed in God reminded me of that, and I kind of thought about it for a minute. I told her that yes, I believed in God, but more importantly, I believed that God believed in me, and it was my opinion that if God was *truly* on the side of the righteous and the disenfranchised, the underdog and the downtrodden, the unprolific and the misunderstood, then He was duty bound to see me, but more precisely, my mother, through the blackest days of our lives, and to show mercy and sympathy where no earthly mercy or sympathy existed. I told her that if it were up to me, I would forgo any obligation God might feel toward me, and instead ask that all such obligations and mercies be extended to my mom—*slunicko moje,* the bravest of the brave, the cheerer of the underdog, the imperfect blanket fort builder, the great storyteller, the blue-eyed runway watcher. I told her I ask God for nothing beyond that.

Margaret took a second and wiped her vulture beak again. I was starting to get a bit nauseous watching her wipe her nose every two seconds with that stink of mothballs hanging all over the goddamn room.

"If I may, Mr. Raskin, I'd like to offer you a prayer, something you certainly look like you could use." She reached over and grabbed my hand. I didn't get a chance to even say anything before she started praying. Not that I would've *stopped* her or anything. If there's one thing I know, it's you can't stop a chaplain from saying a prayer when she wants to say a prayer. It's impossible. You couldn't stop a chaplain from saying a prayer if you were armed to the teeth with every atomic bomb ever made.

When she finished saying her prayer, I thanked her for it. Then I told her I wanted to go to sleep because I'd been up for three days straight and I thought I'd better get some rest so that when it was time for my mom and me to get the hell out of that place, I'd have enough strength to get us as far away from New York as possible.

"Where do you plan to go?" she asked.

"We're going to Lake George. You ever been there? It's about two hundred miles north of here. Up in the Adirondacks. That's where we're going."

"By *we*, you mean you and—"

"My mom. I always promised her, hell or high water, I'd take her there, and we'd hide out in that place before New York City is blown to smithereens in a nuclear terrorist attack."

She didn't say anything for a few minutes. She just sort of sat there and stared at me. I can't stand it when people do that. It's a cheap thing to do, if you ask me. Anyway, instead of sitting there and staring back at her, I fiddled with my October jacket. I pretended to be looking for something in my inside pocket. Luckily, I had a crumpled piece of paper in there—a receipt—and was able to take it out and pretend to be reading it. I was so convincing, in fact, that she eventually asked me if everything was all right. I said it was, and that I was just looking over the receipt to my October jacket. I told her it was a waste of money but was fabulous just the same.

All of a sudden, while she was staring at me, Margaret reached out and sort of put her hand on my shoulder. I was pretty shocked by it, to tell you the truth.

"I'm very sorry for all that you've lost, Michael. My heart breaks for you. No man so young should lose what you have. I—I'm going to let you rest now for a little while, but please know that God will be merciful and will help you if you allow Him to." I kept nodding my head at her, hoping she'd stop already. "I can see it on your face. You don't hide your anguish well."

I thanked her again for the prayer she'd said for my mom, and I told her I'd send for her if I needed her again. I knew I wouldn't, but sometimes the only way to get a social worker off your back is to tell her that you'll probably need her assistance again sometime soon. Anyway, it worked, because she got up and walked out. The one thing she didn't do, though, was close the door behind her. I can't stand it when people do that. You'd think they were all born in a goddamn field or something. I wound up having to get up and put the wood into the hole myself.

For some reason, after I closed the door, the room seemed to get even more ash-gray than it already was. And *colder,* too. I walked back over to my chair and sat down, right next to where my mom was resting.

"Mom?" I said quietly, then reached under the blanket and grabbed her hand. "We are the Dead. Short days ago, We lived, felt dawn, saw sunset glow, Loved and were loved, and now we lie, In Flanders fields."

I stopped to wipe the tears off my face with the sleeve of my October jacket. My mom just lay there with her eyes closed, breathing slowly and loudly, motionless. All of a sudden, while I was wiping my eyes, I noticed a tear dripping from my mom's right eye. I took my finger and gently wiped it away.

I could hardly talk at all. "Don't cry, Mama," I said and wiped her eye again. I couldn't stop crying to save my own life. "God, don't cry. I know you can't talk, I know you can't answer me, Ma, but it's okay. You don't have to, Mama. I know everything you want to say. I love you, too, Ma, and I'm more proud—I'm more proud of you than any boy could ever be. You're a strong, strong person, Ma, and you're going to get your strength back, I know you are, because you and me, we have so many more places left to go. And we can go anywhere we want, Ma—all *sorts* of places. Land's end or the opposite side of Sixty-eighth Drive. It's your choice, Ma. The most reliable car in the world is sitting right outside, right in the parking lot. And we can go *any*where. We're going to get out of here. We're going to get out of this crummy old hospital room and drive straight to Sunday Way. You just give me the word,

Ma. You tell me when you're ready and I'll grab you up out of this lousy goddamn bed and you, me, and little old Del outside will go and—"

I couldn't believe it but my mom started to move her arms. She picked them up and scratched her neck. And then her mouth started to move, like she was cleaning her teeth with her tongue, the way you do when you first wake up in the morning.

"Ma?"

Her mouth kept moving, and she put her arms down.

"Can you hear me, Ma?"

Her head tilted, and then her eyes, with kind of a twitch, opened slowly—very slowly. I got out of my chair and stood over her so she could see me.

"Hey there, Mama," I said, and I ran my hand through her short hair. I tried hard not to let any tears fall out of my eyes and land on her.

She didn't answer me. She just stared at me with her tired, glossy eyes. She looked like she was trying hard to say something.

"Where's Mike?"

"I'm right here, Ma. I'm right here with you." I kept running my hand through her hair.

"Where's Mike?"

"Mom, I'm right here. I've been here with you the whole time, Mama."

She kept staring straight ahead, without even blinking. Then all of a sudden she started whispering.

"Yellow eyes . . . my eyes are yellow . . . yellow eyes . . . my eyes are still yellow . . ."

While she was whispering, I took my October jacket off and wrapped it around her. I made sure to tuck it in tightly around her sides so that it was as snug as possible, so that she wouldn't be cold.

"They're not going to be that way for much longer, Ma, you have to believe that—"

"Yellow eyes . . . my eyes are yellow . . . yellow eyes . . . my eyes are still yellow . . ."

"They won't be anymore, Ma. No more yellow eyes, no more—"

"*Yellow eyes . . .*"

"No more, Ma . . . yellow eyes no more . . . yellow eyes no more . . . yellow eyes no more . . ."

"*Yellow eyes no more . . . yellow eyes no more . . . yellow eyes no more . . .*"

"That's a girl, Ma. *Yellow eyes no more . . . yellow eyes no more . . . yell—*"

"Mr. Raskin?" I heard someone say. I turned around and saw the door opening. It was that pain in the ass again, *Margaret*. "Mr. Raskin, are you okay?"

"What do you mean am I okay? I'm fine. Why wouldn't I be f—"

"Mr. Raskin, why aren't you lying down and resting? You know that's what Dr. Carleton ordered."

"Hey, can't you see I'm in the middle of—"

"C'mon, lie down over here and let's get your vitals. C'mon, Michael."

"For the love of God, Margaret, why do you keep *doing* this to me? You were just in here, for God's sake. Go haunt somebody else, will you?"

"Doctor's orders, Michael. Three times a day. You know the routine by now. Maybe you'd prefer Ms. Thomas to come take your vitals?"

I didn't answer her.

"You sure you're okay?" she asked me again.

I just nodded my head while she took my blood pressure and then my temperature. I'm surprised she didn't give me a goddamn enema while she was at it.

"Okay, you're all set," she said after a few minutes. "Try and get some rest, sweetheart, and please try to *eat* something. Minnie said you haven't eaten a thing in two days. Dr. Carleton will come by to check on you soon. She says you might be going home in a day or two."

"Thou sayeth, Margaret."

She started walking out, taking her stink of mothballs with her. I looked back at my mom, but her eyes were closed again.

"Are you *sure* you're okay, Michael?" Margaret asked me again before she left the room.

I turned around and looked over toward her.

"I'm fine," I said. "I'm fine. I've got a very dear friend here with me and I'm going to be just fine."

Sanctioned by God, Executed by Happenstance

T he note, written in black ink on napkin paper, said:

I believe this is sanctioned by God, Ma. For the time being, I'll miss you more than I can ever describe, more than I know you can ever know, more than any prophetic writer of our time would be able to detail, but I'm going to see you very soon. I know I will. You're a damn orb and I love you for it. Please keep a light on for me.

I set the note down on the gravel and gently slid it over, word-side up, to my mom. I couldn't bring myself to look at her while she read it, so I kept my head down, focusing on the gravel.

Earlier that day—much earlier—just as the dark October clouds were starting to roll in, just as the fall wind was starting to pick up, carrying dead leaves into the air and making street signs sway, we were driving on Route 9, midway between Bolton Landing and Lake George. It was a perfect morning for a drive in the Adirondacks—the type of morning that's impossible to imagine because it's beyond the limits of any honest man's imagination, the type of morning that you'd swear can heal a dying person. It was October jacket weather, jack-o'-lantern weather, messenger bag weather, and, God preserve it, a*non*ymous weather.

I reached over and opened up the glove box, making sure I didn't let it hit my mom's knees as it swung open. I reached in and took out my black newspaper-boy hat that my mom had gotten for me a few years ago from some flea market in New Jersey. She was staying at her brother's house for a few days, I remember, and she came home on a Sunday around midnight. I was asleep in bed. When I woke up in the morning, there was a small shopping bag sitting right next to my pillow, practically touching my nose. When I opened it, I found the hat—a soft wool newspaper-boy hat whose brim was bent just the way I like it, the crease slightly off center but sharp enough so that the brim came down nearly to my eyes, but not *so* low that it would have given me a dizzy spell. The receipt was inside the hat, and on the back, in black marker, was a short note.

October 1 (Halloween month)

Hey Madder (MDR)—

Saw this hat in the Route 18 fleamarket and couldn't resist buying it for you . . . Happy October First! I know how rough the passed few weeks have been on both of us . . . I know how much you hate NYC but let's try and make the best of it O.K.?? Let's do some pumpkin carving this month and watch lots o' scary movies . . . things will get better soon Mike—I promise. If I haven't said it already, thanks for all your help over the last few weeks . . . I'd be dead without you . . . D-E-A-D. Your the best son in the world and I know your dad is looking down on you and beaming with pride . . . he's very proud of you and so am I! Hope this hat keeps you nice and toasty this October and many Octobers to come sonny-boy . . . Love you.

Love,
Mamakin

P.S.—I'm making flounder for dinner tonight . . . will u be home?
P.S.S.—Taking Sunday to get an oil change, then Republic Airport to watch the airplanes . . . be back around 4.

I've carried that newspaper-boy hat around with me ever since, though I've hardly worn it. Whenever I get something nice, I'm always too afraid to use it too much. I'm always worried about it not being the same anymore, about it not being *new* anymore. I usually just wind up keeping it under my pillow so that at night, when the lights are off, I can look at it with a flashlight and think about all the things I *could* be doing with it. That's what I used to do with my newspaper-boy hat. And when I went out during the day, I would always put it in my messenger bag so that I'd have it with me. But the thing is, I hardly ever used it. I hardly ever wore it—maybe *twice,* if I was lucky. I always just liked having it with me. It made me feel safe, and it made me think about my mom walking into the Route 18 flea market and asking the Chinese lady who sold them all sorts of sizing questions. That always gave me a charge. Anyway, what I should really start doing is buying *two* of everything. One to use and one to keep around just to look at after the other one gets dirty.

Either way, like I was saying, I took my newspaper-boy hat out of the glove box and put it on. I made sure not to pull it down so low that it obstructed my vision because I was keeping my eyes open for Grandma's Back Porch Restaurant. I knew it was located right on Route 9, not too far from where we were, but because it was October I wasn't banking on their sign being displayed. These resort towns never keep their signs out in the fall.

My mom had her seat reclined—or as much as a del Sol's seat reclines—and her red fleece blanket draped over her. I couldn't see her face, but I knew she was sleeping. I reached over and tousled her hair a bit. With both of our windows rolled down a few inches, her hair was being tossed around gently by the wind, knotting in some places and straightening in others. I tried to get some knots out, and then just kept my hand on top of her head.

I was right not to count on Grandma's having their sign displayed. It was covered with some sort of tarp, and I only recognized the turn because of a scarecrow at the foot of Hill Road—the road that leads into the parking lot—with a small handwritten sign on it saying that Grandma's was closed for the season. I was disappointed as all hell, to tell you the truth, but I didn't bother to wake my mom or anything. Instead, I just pulled into the parking lot and took a spot.

"We're here, Ma," I said very quietly, though I knew she wasn't going to be able to answer me. I looked over at her, and she still had her fleece blanket on with her back toward me, still breathing hard and slow. Even though Grandma's was closed, I didn't feel very much like leaving the parking lot. I really couldn't think of any other place to go. So all I did was tilt my seat back and close my eyes. I took my October jacket off and pulled it over me as if it were a blanket, and I left my newspaper-boy hat on.

I couldn't help thinking about something that happened a couple of summers ago. It was the first time my mom and I had ever been to Grandma's, and we were sitting at a table on the porch, looking out at Hill Road and the lake. It was early—just past nine-thirty—and it was one of those mornings that was so nice, so warm, and so anonymous, it made you feel lousy because every day wasn't as nice. In a lot of ways, it was a crummy morning.

"That's all you're going to have, a glass of cranberry juice?" my mom, sitting across from me, said.

"I don't like to eat anything heavy before getting back on the road," I told her.

"That's ridiculous, Mike. You know you're getting very skinny. You're starting to look a little—"

"*Ma*, would you knock it off, huh? It's too early to get into this. Why don't you just take it easy and—"

"I'm just *saying* you might *feel* better if you *ate* something, that's all."

"And all *I'm* saying is I might feel better if you didn't *hassle* me about it, Ma."

I took a drink of cranberry juice and then went back to staring at the lake. My mom had her sunglasses on and her right arm resting on the railing of the porch. I remember how the water looked that morning. It was reflecting so much sun you could hardly look at it without squinting.

"Makes me sick to my stomach that we have to go back to Queens today," I said after a few minutes.

"For God's sake, spare me the speech this morning,

Mike, *please*. You say the same damn thing every time we—"

"Well I can't help it, all right? My disdain for that city is such that you couldn't measure it if you tried, Ma. I *literally* get *phys*ically sick when I think about going back there. All that congestion and filth and construction and ten-dollar-a-gallon gas, it makes me want to puke. I don't know how the hell you can say you actually *like*—"

"Oh, *please*. You know perfectly well I don't *like* it there. But I don't com*plain* about it twenty-four hours a day like you do, and talk about nuclear bombs going off and all sorts of terrible things. You know, the problem with you, my darling son, is you just can't let yourself be happy for *five* minutes. You spend more time on vacation than *any*-body I know. I mean, I realize you've been dealt a bad blow in life, both of us have, but it is what it is, and if we don't try and make the best of the predicament we're in, then we're not going to just be *miserable,* we're going to both be *dead.* I mean, look at me. Just think about this for a second, will you? I've got one foot in the grave already, but do you think I'm going to let that stop me from doing the things I like to do, like coming to Lake George and spending time with you, playing miniature golf at Pirate's Cove and eating all sorts of really good food? Hell no! H-E double hockey sticks *no*. So why can't you just try and enjoy—"

"Look," I said, "would you stop with that business of having one foot in the grave. If you have one foot in the grave then I must have a foot and a half, because I can't think a goddamn thought these days without feeling like jumping off a cliff, and I'll tell you a thing or two about—"

"Oh, that's a *real* nice thing for you to say, Mike, especially with all that's going on with me. You feel like jumping off a cliff. *Very* nice."

"All I meant, Ma, is that I—"

"You what?"

"I can't stop thinking that *all* this—all of this, this whole place here, everything you see, this nice porch with all these people, this perfect weather, that road down there, that *lake*, you and me sitting together and talking about things the way I like—I can't stop thinking that all of this is going to be another one of my memories someday, Ma, another one of my memories that I think about at night, that I stay up all night thinking about and wanting nothing more than to be able to go back and spend one more minute—no, one more *second,* even—there again. I can't stop thinking that it's all going to be memories, and I want to tell you something about memories—"

"*Mike*—"

"Wait awhile, try not to interrupt me here for a minute, Ma. The only good goddamn thing about memories is that they remind you you're still alive, that you're still active duty. But if you're looking for something be*yond* that, you might as well wait for Jesus Christ because there isn't anything. Nothing. Memories are a prelude to mental breakdown and suicide."

"*Suicide?* Have you lost your mind, Mike? I mean, give me a break already. You think I'd even be *alive* today, with all I'm going through, if I didn't have all those wonderful memories of your father to think about? I mean, *seriously.*

If I didn't have the wherewithal, as *you* would say, to think about all those times we spent in Maine together, all those camping trips we went on, all those drives to the country we made—you, me, Dad and Cleo—I'd have checked myself out a *long* time ago. You think *memories* lead to suicide? You've got it backwards, pal. Having *no* memories leads to suicide."

I didn't say anything for a few minutes. I just sat there and stared out at the lake, watching the sailboats and the occasional speedboat go by. Eventually, the waitress came by and sort of brightened things up. Her name was Sarah, and, to be as frank as possible, she was drop-dead gorgeous, in a plain Jane sort of way. In *my* sort of way.

"Y'all set over here?" she asked.

"Would you tell my son to lighten up a bit, Sarah," my mom said. "Tell him that girls don't like sourpusses."

"*Ma*—" I said, and I couldn't help but laugh. Sarah had a look on her face that was goddamn priceless.

"No, seriously," my mom said. "He's mad because he has

to go home today. Tell him he'll feel better if he has something to eat."

"Mama knows best," Sarah said. I could tell she was
embarrassed as hell. She had a real embarrassed smile on
her face. "Where are y'all from?"

I looked up and rolled my eyes. "Queens," I said.

"He hates it," my mom said. "He wants to buy a house
up here but I keep telling him he's got champagne taste
and a beer budget."

"Well, I guess there's nothing the matter with aiming
high," Sarah said and looked over at me.

"You see that, Ma?" I said. "She's knows what she's
talking about."

My mom laughed. "I'll be a son of a gun but you two are
perfect for each other. Sarah, are you single?"

"*Ma*, for *God's* sake."

"*What?* I'm just asking her if she's single, for crying out
loud."

Sarah's face was redder than a damn tomato and she
was laughing so hard she was just about crying. Before

my mother had another chance to embarrass me, I jumped in and told Sarah not to pay my mom any mind because she had a couple of kangaroos loose in the top paddock. I wasn't very effective, though, because as soon as I stopped talking, my mom told Sarah to bring me three egg whites, wheat toast, and another glass of cranberry juice.

I didn't say anything about it. To tell you the truth, I was starting to like Sarah so much I would've eaten *ten* plates of egg whites and toast if it meant spending more time with her.

"All right, screw it," I finally said. "Bring me some breakfast."

"Your mama's looking out for you," Sarah said before she walked off.

"Yeah," I said. "She's always looking out for me."

While I was sitting in the car with my mom in the empty parking lot, with my October jacket covering me and the dead leaves scurrying all around us, I couldn't stop thinking about that stuff. I couldn't stop thinking about it

thinking to himself that if this was as good as it got, if this was the only way a writer could make money writing—by writing substandard catalog copy—then perhaps writing with money as motivation really wasn't writing at all, and if it wasn't, then the only way to be a *real* writer was to write with *nothing* as motivation, nothing except the desire to *tell*.

While I was looking at the brochure and reading it, I heard a girl say "*Hey, Dylan.*" I looked up and saw Jody—the owner—standing behind the desk. She looked particularly good that day, too. She must've been in her thirties, but she looked younger. Her hair was blonde, and it had these really terrific dark streaks in it, but not the kind that look dyed-in.

"*Jody*, what's happening, ace?" I said.

"Not too bad," she said. I got a kick out of that one. "You know I didn't recognize you for a second. What'd you do, cut all your hair off?"

"Yeah, I lost a goddamn bet."

She laughed and then started typing on the computer. I

figured she was probably bringing up my file. I told her I needed a room for the night.

"Are you here with your mom or by yourself?"

"With my mom. She's out in the car sleeping off the long ride."

Jody registered us and said she'd be putting us in our favorite room, which was room 143. That was the room we always stayed in. We liked it because it was the last room on the end of the second floor, and it was always pretty quiet. I thanked her and told her I'd give her my mom's credit card when we checked out the next day.

"You going into town to check out the action today?" she asked as I was walking out.

"I'm sorry?" I said.

"There's a bit of an event happening at Jitters Café this afternoon. You might want to go check it out."

I thanked her again and told her I would.

"Everything all right, Dylan?" Jody said as I was holding open the door, trying to leave. "You don't look so well. You're looking a little pale."

"Just tired from the drive, that's all, Jo. I'll feel better after I lie down a little, get some food in me and everything."

She said something else as I was walking away, but I couldn't make it out too clearly. Anyway, I took a quick sprint over to where the car was and opened up the passenger door. My mom still had her fleece blanket covering her. I kneeled down and ran my hand through her hair a few times.

"Mama?" I said very softly. "C'mon, Mama, let's get you upstairs."

There were two double beds in room 143, and I helped my mom into the bed furthest from the window and closest to the water closet. I moved all the motel sheets and everything and just covered her with her red fleece blanket. I made sure I tucked it in underneath her so that she was wrapped up as tightly as possible.

"Mom, I'm just going to run into town for a while, okay? I'll score us some food and bring it back here in a little while. You just rest now, Mama. I'll come back soon and we'll go into town together, all right? All right, Ma?"

She didn't answer me and I knew she wouldn't. I leaned over and kissed her on the head and told her I'd be right back.

It was a breezy and overcast October afternoon, just the way I like them, so I decided to walk into town instead of driving. It was too damn nice out not to walk. I had my October jacket on and my messenger bag with me, and I started out walking north on Route 9. Because it was the fall, there really weren't that many cars around. There were hardly any *people,* let alone cars. It was nicer that way, though. It was more anonymous, and it made the town feel like a cemetery. It reminded me, in a way, of what October used to be like when I was a kid. There was hardly a day in October, when I was a kid, that all of Queens didn't feel like a cemetery. It was always overcast and shadowy out, and the streets, particularly in the late afternoon, were always very deserted and desolate, and the only noise you ever heard, practically, were all the leaves blowing across the sidewalks and the gutters. You always *knew* it was October. It always *felt* like October. There were always a lot of Halloween decorations and things everywhere you looked, and there were always little kids running around trick-or-treating, even on *school* nights. It was October and you *knew* it was October. It hasn't been that obvious since.

Walking down Route 9 in Lake George sort of reminded me of those days. By the time I made it to the village, I'd put my newspaper-boy hat back on my head. It made me feel safe. It made me feel anonymous. Just as I was about to cross the street to see if I could score myself a slice of pizza from Pizza Jerks, a girl came running up alongside me. She damn near gave me heart failure.

"Darryl?" she asked.

I recognized her right away. I'd met her the summer before outside of a store called the Silvermine. She was sitting outside on a bench wearing a pair of cargo pants and eating a bagel, and I stopped to ask her where she'd gotten it. Her name was Melissa, and she was a bit of all right, if only slightly out of her box. She was very hyperactive.

Anyway, I was surprised as hell to see her. She looked damn good, too. She was wearing a nice pair of cargo pants—just like the first time I saw her—and her hair was pulled back in a ponytail. She was waify and sort of homeless looking. She looked like a painter.

"Hey, Meliss," I said. I didn't bother correcting her about my name. "How've you b—"

"What are you *doing* here? Are you here with your mom?" She jumped on me and gave me a hug before I could get out a word. I told you she was a hyperactive son of a bitch.

"*Yeah,*" I said. "We just came up for the day, seeing as it's October and—"

"*Oh,* you *have* to come to Jitters with me! Is that why you came up? How'd you hear about it?"

"Huh? Hear about what?"

"A friend of mine is autographing his books there today. You've got to come! They're about to start in a few minutes, you've got to come."

Melissa was looking very excited and had a big ole smile on her face. I thought for a minute she was stoned on something.

"You mean it's a goddamn *book* signing?" I said.

"He should be starting any minute. C'mon, Darryl, come with me! He's a friend of mine and he's really talented. You'll have a good time." She started grabbing at the sleeve of my October jacket and kept bouncing around like she had a spring or two underneath her feet.

If there's one thing I really can't stand, it's a book signing. In my opinion they shouldn't even be allowed to exist. When I read a book, the *last* thing I want is to meet its author and hear what the poor bastard sounds like in person. It ruins the whole damn book for me. All of a sudden, I start *hearing* it differently. I start hearing it the same way the author sounds in person. I hate that. I hate that more than anything. I *especially* hate it when I read a book that has some edge to it, and then I see the author on television or somewhere and he turns out to be some mousy guy in a cheap brown suit. It can make me never want to read another book again in my life.

But anyway, what the hell could I say to her? I knew if I told her I was out looking to get some food she would've just told me that Jitters has some of the best damn food in town. Plus, I figured if this book signing was some kind of big event in Lake George, Jacksonville from the Village Mall or Danielle from Mike & Don's Waterfront Café might be there.

So I told Melissa I'd go, and we both started walking over toward Jitters. It was located right in the Mayard Center, just off Canada Street. The minute we got there, though, I knew I'd made a big mistake. Every one of Melissa's goddamn friends was there—every single one. I'm not exaggerating. And, naturally, as soon as we walked in, every last one of them came running over to say hello to her. And the whole time they were taking turns hugging each other and everything, they kept batting around inside jokes and laughing up a goddamn storm. I was beginning to feel like a royal horse's ass standing there. So I kept looking around to see if Jacksonville or Danielle were in attendance, but of course they weren't. Goddamn girls. They're never around when you want them to be around.

Finally, after Melissa finished making the rounds

with her friends, she started introducing me to every bastard and his brother. And she kept introducing me as *Darryl*. "Rachel, this is my friend *Darryl*. Hey, Bobby, this is my friend *Darryl*." *Darryl* this and *Darryl* that. She must've introduced me to *fifty* people as Darryl. It was quite a situation.

Anyway, we sat down at a table that was practically on *top* of the goddamn microphone. The author wasn't there yet, so we had to wait a good ten minutes before the son of a bitch showed up. But when he did, you never heard a small crowd yell and whistle so loud in your entire life. I'm not exaggerating. I could hardly hear myself curse, the way these people were yelling. They kept screaming out the guy's name, but I couldn't make it out.

It was funny. The minute he got in front of the microphone, he sat down on a stool and started reading from his book. He didn't bother saying hello or thanks for coming or anything. He just sat down and started reading. Some things I don't remember too clearly. I can't remember anything about what he read because I wasn't paying all that much attention. All I remember is that he kept reading, and after every sentence—every single one—he'd sort of take his face out of his stinking book for a second and give someone in the crowd a wink. Especially the parts that were all about sex and drugs and things. And almost every other word was a curse word. *F* this and *F* that. And just about every time he read a curse word, someone in the crowd would either whistle or cheer like an idiot. I didn't give a damn for him as a writer, to be perfectly honest with you. He struck me as the kind of guy who kept a scrapbook about himself, the kind of guy who gave his own book out as a gift. Typical big shot.

I don't remember how long I had to sit there, but by the time it was over my teeth were floating. I had to piss so bad I was farting, and I still hadn't gotten a chance to eat anything. So I went up to the counter and bought an oatmeal-raisin cookie, my favorite kind next to peanut butter. It damn near cost a double sawbuck, but I figured it would hold me over until I got back to the motel. Anyway, I took my cookie back over to the table and sat down. I didn't see

Melissa anywhere, so I figured I'd just eat my oatmeal-raisin cookie and then head back over to the motel to check on my mom. But before I could even take two bites of the damn thing, Melissa came over and took my newspaper-boy hat off my head, in a very playful sort of way.

"Do I look like you?" she said as she put on my newspaper-boy hat.

"Well maybe if you tuck your—"

"*HEYYY,* baby!" she yelled all of a sudden. She was talking to the big-shot author. They started hugging right away. "You did *great,* baby!" she kept saying to him. I got a kick out of that one.

"*Darryl,* hey," Melissa yelled over to me. "I want you to meet my *super* talented friend, Jon."

"Darryl?" he asked and shook my hand. "Jon, with no *h.*" I hate it when people say things like that. Especially when you have a common-as-muck name like *Jon.*

"Darryl, with no *e,*" I said. I had a hard time keeping a straight face after that one. "You did a good job up there, ace."

"Thanks a lot, buddy. I had a real good time." *Buddy*— that one gave me a charge. I can't stand it when people I've never met before call me *buddy*.

Then, all of a sudden, Jon got this look in his eye like he was about to bang on about something. I can always tell when one of these big shots is getting ready to bang on about something. I was immediately sorry I'd said anything to the son of a bitch.

"Yeah, I really love to write," he said. "It's my passion in life. And I like to read my work to people, too, so I feel pretty fortunate that I get to do this for a living. I mean, it's what I *love* to do."

That one was about as hot as a neutron bomb. These blowhards are always giving you a lot of who shot Johnny about how much they love their goddamn life. I had a hard time not going into hysterics, but I wound up not saying anything at all. It was useless anyway. It's no wonder he and Melissa got along so well. Both of them could talk without coming up for air.

"This is my first book, so I'm pretty stoked about it. I've

always been a fan of first books so this is pretty earth-shaking for me."

Earth-shaking. I loved that one. The way he said it sort of reminded me of these big-shot suburban guys who move to Brooklyn and talk all the suburban girls into bed with their artsy talk. In any case, I didn't bother straightening him out. I didn't want to burst his goddamn bubble or anything.

"I wish you the best," I said to him. I shook the bastard's hand and then went over to Melissa to try and get my newspaper-boy hat back. She was busy shooting the wind with some of her friends. I had to kind of sneak up behind her and rip it off her head.

"*Darryl!*" she said. "Are you leaving me?"

I pointed to my watch and told her I had to get back to my motel because I had to spend a penny, that I'd been holding it in since the morning. Her friends were looking at me like I was out of my mind. I put my hat on and told her I was sure I'd see her soon because I was planning on buying a house in town. I got a big kick out of that.

Anyway, she came over and gave me a hug and told me to stop into the Silvermine the next time I was in town. I guess she worked there or something. I told her I'd be sure to, and I left.

It was very shadowy and desolate out when I left the Mayard Center. Canada Street didn't have a single person on it, and nearly every store in the village—even the ones that were *closed* for the season—had a pumpkin in its window. It was breezy out, so I flipped the collar on my October jacket up and adjusted my newspaper-boy hat to make it fit just the way I like it.

Some things aren't easy to remember. I couldn't tell you precisely when it hit me, but not long after I'd left the Mayard Center, right there on Canada Street, my heart started racing out of control, and the only thing I could think about was my mom. All of a sudden, I couldn't stop thinking about her. I couldn't stop *worrying* about her, and I got this terrific feeling of guilt about leaving her by herself, about not being able to help her feel better, about not being able to let her live the way she *deserved* to live, about monopolizing her and keeping her from spending time with all the other people who loved and missed her, about her feeling scared and alone, unsure if she should stay or leave.

My heart started pounding so hard that I had to go and lay down on a bench. I thought I might have a heart attack. In fact, I was *positive* that I was going to have one. The knot in my neck hurt so much I could hardly talk, but I started to ask for help anyway.

"*Please*, Dad," I kept saying. "*Please,* Daddy. Please help me. Show me the way. I'm trying so hard, Dad, but I can't make it out here. I'm lost, Dad. I'm in the middle of nowhere and I'm out of places to go, and I've got nobody left. No one. Please show me the way. Heal me, Dad. Please come and heal me, give me the strength to get right in the head, to order my steps. I need you. *Please,* Daddy."

I could hardly bring myself to move, so I just lay there in my October jacket and newspaper-boy hat for a good while until my heart started to slow down a little. While I lay there I could feel dead leaves blowing around me and scraping against my dungarees. I didn't bother to move any of them away.

I'm not sure when it was that I sat up, but when I did I remember feeling like I wasn't going to be able to make it all the way back to the motel. So I just sat there for a few minutes and looked around at all the deserted streets and all the leaves blowing around. It was October and it *felt* like October. For the first time in a very long time, it felt like October. I had a marker in the inside pocket of my jacket, and I took it out and wrote a short note on a piece of paper I'd taken from Jitters. I folded it over three times and stuffed it in my inside pocket where I knew I wouldn't lose it. Then I got up and started walking.

Walking up Route 9 back to the Super 8 was rather arduous, but I felt a little better when I made it back to my room. My mom was just where I'd left her, still in the bed furthest from the window and closest to the water closet, still wrapped tightly in her red fleece blanket. I went over and sat on the edge of my bed and watched her lying there for a few minutes. I didn't say anything. I just sat there and watched her.

By the time five o'clock came around, the fall wind had picked up considerably, and as we drove down Route 9, Lake George seemed more ash-gray than shadowy, more campground than cemetery. We drove past Rosie's Diner, just beyond the entrance to the thruway, past Grandma's Back Porch Restaurant, and turned right onto a quiet, leaf-covered gravel road that cracked and popped under our wheels. I stopped the car in the middle of the road and turned off the engine. It was so quiet my ears popped when I opened the door. I got out and adjusted my news-paper-boy hat, and then I walked around the back of the car and let my mom out. I kept my arm around her, and we both went and sat right in the middle of the road, right on the gravel.

Neither of us said anything for a little while. We just sat there and let the wind rustle our clothes and make our eyes tear. It was so quiet out, except for the wind and the scraping leaves, you would swear the rest of the world was dead. I couldn't think of anything proper to say, so I reached out and put my arm around my mom. I pulled her close and cradled her head, making sure the zipper on my October jacket didn't scratch her face.

"Oh, Mama," I said and kissed the top of her head. "My sweet, sweet Mama. *I want to feel high like I did back then when time passed slowly, and a friend was still a friend, and I want you to be just what you said you'd be to me, always right beside me 'til the very end, and I want to paint skies, I want to leave time, feel with my hands, let my eyes be blind.*" I stopped for a minute and looked around, then put my hand through my mom's short, floppy hair, and told her goodbye.

I let my mom go and unzipped my October jacket. I reached into my inside pocket and unfolded the piece of paper I had in there and looked it over.

The note, written in black ink on napkin paper, said:

I believe this is sanctioned by God, Ma. For the time being, I'll miss you more than I can ever describe, more than I know you can ever know, more than any prophetic writer of our time would be able to detail, but I'm going to see you very soon. I know I will. You're a damn orb and I love you for it. Please keep a light on for me.

I set the note down on the gravel and gently slid it over, word-side up, to my mom. I couldn't bring myself to look at her while she read it, so I kept my head down, focusing on the gravel.

M ike?" Dr. Millani said.

I kind of scratched the back of my head and looked at her.

"I don't really feel like getting into it," I finally said. "I've just been shuffling around a lot, thinking about things and remembering stuff."

She didn't say anything for a minute. She sort of put her elbows back on the table, interlocked her fingers and rested her chin on her hands and stared at me.

"Do you remember what I told you a while back, about how I felt after my dad died?" she asked me. "The one thing I struggled with, the one thing that I couldn't quite get my mind around, was how he had to live with his cancer, the way this man just fell apart before my eyes and—I don't know if you remember that I told you—he died in my arms."

"I remember," I said.

"Right. Well, my point is, I've had to live with that. But what sort of happened over time is I started dwelling a little less on how sick he was, and about what he had to go through living with this horrible disease, and I started remembering him for who he was be*fore* cancer." She was looking like she might be on the verge of crying. I'd seen her cry before, and she was looking that way again.

"Did I ever tell you that I remember the first time you came to the hospital with your mom after she started chemotherapy? It was the first time you walked in after you'd cut your hair off. Do you remember I asked you why you did that, and you said you did it because you thought it'd make things easier for your mom if you both looked a little funny for a while?"

I nodded my head yes. Dr. Millani let her arms down and rested them on the table.

"I don't know if I'm saying the right things here, Mike. I just care a lot about you, I really do, and I don't want you to spend the rest of your life agonizing over what your mom went through. I know it's only been a couple of months since the funeral, but are you still thinking about it constantly? Are you still thinking of her as she was those last couple weeks?"

"I can't always help the way I think of her," I said.

Dr. Millani paused for a minute and put her hand to her face, then wiped her eyes.

"You know that you can take her with you everywhere you go," she said.

"I *do* take her with me everywhere I go."

We both sat there for a little while without saying anything.

"Thank you for seeing me, Dr. Millani," I finally said.

"Oh, don't call me Dr. Millani." She got up out of her chair.

I sort of laughed a little. "Thank you for seeing me, Tina."

Dr. Millani came over and gave me a hug.

"Can I adopt you or something?" she asked me.

I laughed slightly. "You wouldn't know what to do with

me," I said. Then I thanked her for all she did for my mom—*and* for me. I told her she was as reliable as a Honda.

"Look," I said, after we let go. "I can't *force* you to leave, but I'm begging you to get out of New York before it's too late, before a nuclear—"

She kind of laughed.

"I'll be fine," she said. "What about you? Where're you planning on going?"

"I'm going to go to a place where I can spend some time with my parents."

Driving out of New York that morning, it was clear as could be that October was well gone—off somewhere, way out of range. The traffic was heavy and the wind was blowing papers into the air and scarf tips into faces. I pulled into a filling station and took a spot next to the gas pumps. My newspaper-boy hat was in my messenger bag, and I took it out. I took some lint off of it, then put it on, letting it fall just below my eyebrows, the brim obstructing my view, leaving nothing at all to see.